SYNCHRONICITY

SYNCHRONICITY

THE INNER
PATH OF
LEADERSHIP

Introduction by Peter Senge

JOSEPH JAWORSKI

BETTY SUE FLOWERS, EDITOR

Berrett-Koehler Publishers
San Francisco

Berrett-Koehler Publishers, Inc.
450 Sansome St., Suite 1200
San Francisco, CA 94111-3320
Tel: (415) 288-0260, Fax: (415) 362-2512

Ordering Information
Individual sales. Berrett-Koehler publications are available through most bookstores. They can also be ordered direct from Berrett-Koehler at the address above.

Quantity sales. Special discounts are available on quantity purchases by corporations, associations, and others. For details, contact the "Special Sales Department" at the Berrett-Koehler address above.

Orders for college textbook/course adoption use. Please contact Berrett-Koehler Publishers at the address above.

Orders by U.S. trade bookstores and wholesalers. Please contact Publishers Group West, 4065 Hollis St., Box 8843, Emeryville, CA 94662. Tel. (510) 658-3453; 1-800-788-3123; fax (510) 658-1834.

Printed in the United States of America

 Printed on acid-free and recycled paper that is composed of 85% recovered fiber, including 15% postconsumer waste.

Library of Congress Cataloging-in-Publication Data
Jaworski, Joseph, 1934-
    Synchronicity : the inner path of leadership / Joseph Jaworski ; Betty Sue Flowers, editor.
      p. cm.
    ISBN 1-57675-031-0 (paperback alk. paper)
    ISBN 1-881052-94-X (hardcover alk. paper)
    1. Self-realization. 2. Leadership. 3. Success. 4. Organizational learning.
5. Jaworski, Joseph, 1934-   .
I. Flowers, Betty S. II. Title.
BJ1470.J38 1996
158'.4--dc20

96-948
CIP

First Hardcover Printing: April 1996
First Paperback Printing: January 1998

05 04 03 02 01 00 99 98   10 9 8 7 6 5 4 3 2

"I've spent my life writing about a new way to think and to be. Joe Jaworski has spent his living it. His deeply personal vision of Servant Leadership, nurtured by a courageous openness to love, to pain, and to his own and others' experience, is told with a profound simplicity. *Synchronicity* touched deeply both my head and my heart."

—**Danah Zohar,** author of *Rewiring the Corporate Brain,*
The Quantum Self, and *The Quantum Society*

"From seemingly simple early chords, this book develops into a prophetic symphony by its conclusion."

—**M. Scott Peck**

"An unusually thoughtful exploration of the 'inner' aspects of leadership, particularly in the business arena, surfaces in Joseph Jaworski's *Synchronicity.* Eschewing easy answers and ten-point plans to success, presenting the insights he has garnered from forward-looking thinkers including David Bohm and Rupert Sheldrake, Jaworski offers a searching and wise brief that deserves to be read in boardrooms everywhere."

—*Publishers Weekly*

"No other book is like this one. Its gripping life stories punctuate a how-to on managing toward 'predictable miracles' by exploring your 'cubic centimeters of chance.' What a wake-up call!"—**Tom Brown's Top Ten Business Books of 1996**

"Joseph Jaworski pinpoints the astonishing encounters which manifested in his life when he followed his inner compass. Wise guides rose spontaneously; fate cleared blockages; love was caught in an airport passing; even an ermine communed eye-to-eye. Jaworski's life story teaches us how to recognize and respond to our own moments of inner knowing and how these personal shifts can reverberate in the world."

—**Lois Farfel Stark,** American Leadership Forum Fellow, and President,
Stark Productions, Inc.

TO MY FATHER
WHO LED BY EXAMPLE

CONTENTS

PREFACE

We've all had those perfect moments, when things come together in an almost unbelievable way, when events that could never be predicted, let alone controlled, remarkably seem to guide us along our path. The closest I've come to finding a word for what happens in these moments is "synchronicity." C. G. Jung's classic, "Synchronicity: An Acausal Connecting Principle," defines synchronicity as "a meaningful coincidence of two or more events, where something other than the probability of chance is involved." In the beautiful flow of these moments, it seems as if we are being helped by hidden hands. I have often had such seemingly accidental experiences, both in business and in my personal life, and have always been highly intrigued by them, wondering how they occurred. Over the years my curiosity has grown, particularly about how these experiences occur *collectively* within a group or team of people. I have come to see this as the most subtle territory of leadership, creating the conditions for "predictable miracles."

My quest to understand synchronicity arose out of a series of events in my life that led me into a process of inner transformation. As a result of this transformation I decided to follow a dream that I had held close to my heart for a number of years. It was the most difficult decision I had ever made, but the day I made it, I crossed a threshold. From that moment on, what happened to me had the most mysterious quality about it. Things began falling into place almost effortlessly, and I began to discover remarkable people who were to provide crucial assistance to me. This lasted for over a year. Then I lost the flow and almost destroyed the dream I had worked so hard to establish. Ultimately I regained the capacity to participate in what I later came to understand as an unfolding creative order.

These experiences led me to search for the meaning behind extraordinary moments in time. Why did so many doors open for me after I crossed the threshold? How did I lose the capacity to create the future I had envisioned? How did I regain that capacity? What principles could be discerned from these experiences? If this dynamic occurs in individuals, why can't it occur collectively in organizations and even societies as well? What qualities of leadership could inspire this dynamic to occur?

I am the first to acknowledge that in attempting to address these questions we are exploring the frontiers of human knowledge, and that whatever is said here is only a beginning. But this is the story of my personal journey in search of the answers to those questions, and of my inner transformation along the way. I invite you to take that journey with me. Along the way, you will meet some of the people who are leading the renaissance now occurring in many disciplines: philosophy, physics, neurobiology, leadership theory, and organizational learning. These people are breaking the boundaries between disparate disciplines and transforming them at their furthest reaches—where for me they all converge, leading to a deeper understanding of how human beings, both individually and collectively, might develop the capacity to see what wants to emerge in this world and thus have the opportunity to shape the future instead of simply responding to the forces at large.

This book is organized in four parts that track the journey Joseph Campbell describes in *The Hero with a Thousand Faces*. Campbell presents a composite picture of the heroic quest, which is an archetype of the change process humans and, I suggest, organizations alike can pass through. Even though this is my story, I don't intend it to be an autobiography. To the contrary, it's intended to be everybody's story; that's why I've referred to my family members—who have played such crucial roles in my own journey—only when it is essential to the story itself. As Campbell pointed out, the hero's journey is the journey of any of us who elect to search for our true destiny. It reflects the inevitable passages we encounter as we discover how to create the future. We hardly have the language to describe the fundamental shift of mind that permits us to participate in this unfolding creative order. A story is the most powerful way, indeed, the *only* way I know to begin.

I have intentionally written this book in a way to embody the journey itself, so that the earlier chapters represent the level of consciousness I experienced at that particular point in time. The best way I know to carry the reader into the journey itself is to echo for the reader what I was actually experiencing. I struggled with this decision because some of the incidents in the earlier chapters are not very flattering. Yet all of our experiences form an essential part of our developmental path, helping to shape us into what we are in the process of becoming. In that sense, as I look back, I am less judgmental about those earlier days. I encourage you to do likewise as you consider your own journey.

The story begins with "Preparing to Journey," a description of the inauthentic life and the call to adventure which comes in many ways, both subtle and explicit. It is the call to become what we were meant to become, the call to achieve our vital design. Part Two, "Crossing the Threshold," describes the moment of decision, when we say "yes" to the call to adventure. If we have truly committed to follow our dream, we will find that a powerful force exists beyond ourselves and our conscious will, a force that helps us along the way, nurturing our quest and transformation. Part Three tells of "The Hero's Journey," the inevitable supreme ordeal which tests our commitment to the direction we have taken and offers us the opportunity to learn from our failures. The final section, "The Gift," describes the story of the quest accomplished and what it has brought both to individuals and to society as a whole. Here I describe the process of transformation on the journey.

Peter Senge's introduction is designed to be a sort of road map for the reader. Senge is the author of the pathbreaking book, *The Fifth Discipline*, which caused a worldwide groundswell of interest in learning organizations. For the past fifteen years, Senge and a number of his colleagues at MIT have been working to understand how to move organizations along the path of learning. They believe that the essence of a learning organization involves not only the development of new capacities, but also fundamental shifts of mind, individually and collectively—the very shifts that are the subject of this book. Nothing of real substance happens, they say, without this kind of transformation. Given this interest in transformation and how it can be most effectively led, it seemed appropriate to ask Peter to write the introduction. I also had a more personal reason for requesting this of him. As Peter explains in the introduction, he was deeply involved in helping me to write the book, and he was present with me almost the entire time as I made the journey toward wholeness that I describe within these pages.

It only remains for me to tell you about the serious reservations I have had about writing and publishing this book. How could I begin to tell others about the journey toward personal transformation when I find myself so often caught in my own shortcomings? I found a great deal of comfort in reading Henri J. M. Nouwen's book *Reaching Out*. Nouwen said that for a long time he hesitated to write that book, but that he had found consolation and encouragement in the words of seventh-century ascetic, John of the Ladder:

> If some are still dominated by their former bad habits, and yet can teach by mere words, let them teach. . . . For perhaps, by being put to shame by their own words, they will eventually begin to practice what they teach.

I hope that this book will serve you in your own personal transformation and that you will come to an even deeper understanding than is revealed here of how these predictable miracles might occur in your life, in the leadership of your organization, and in society as a whole.

Joseph Jaworski
Hamilton, Massachusetts
February 1996

ACKNOWLEDGMENTS

This book traces a journey that spans two decades of my life. Along the way, I have met the most remarkable people who added important new dimensions to my understanding and to my life. Many are mentioned among the pages of this book, but others are not. To all of them, I express my deepest and most heartfelt gratitude.

I owe an additional debt of gratitude:

• To my partners at Bracewell and Patterson, who have continued to build the firm with integrity and excellence. Our deep bonds of friendship, which were forged during the early years of building the firm, remain today.

• To the American Leadership Forum national trustees and the local chapter founders and executive directors, who served over the years and who devoted their commitment, energy, and resources to the enterprise. I wish to particularly acknowledge Dennis Mullane and Harry F. Merrow, Chairman and Executive Director respectively of the very first independent American Leadership Forum Chapter. They had the courage and foresight to step forward in the earliest days and acted as my mentors and guides throughout my tenure with the Forum.

• To the staff of the American Leadership Forum national office and the Executive Ventures Group, with whom I was privileged to be associated.

• To all the American Leadership Forum fellows with whom I worked, and whose growth and development served to inform and illuminate my own.

• To Peter Senge and Betty Sue Flowers, who were my collaborators on this book. But for their dedication and deep caring, this book would never have been completed.

• To Charles and Beth Miller, who generously provided encouragement and the opportunity to write in the inspirational setting of their home in Santa Fe, New Mexico.

• To my wife, Mavis, and my children, Joe S., Leon, and Shannon, for the care, interest, understanding, and moral support they provided over the years I worked on this manuscript.

• And finally, to my executive assistants, Mary Dabney and Sheila Sutton, and to Cinde Hastings, for their dedication and valuable support throughout the process of this work.

INTRODUCTION

by Peter Senge

TELLING A STORY

For many years I have told people that although there are a lot of books on leadership, there is only one that serious students have to read—*Servant Leadership* by Robert K. Greenleaf. Most recent books on leadership have been about what leaders do and how they operate, why the world makes life difficult for them, and what organizations must do in order to better develop leaders. These books are packed with seemingly practical advice about what individuals and organizations should do differently. Yet few penetrate to deeper insights into the nature of real leadership. By contrast, Greenleaf invites people to consider a domain of leadership grounded in a state of being, not doing. He says that the first and most important choice a leader makes is the choice to serve, without which one's capacity to lead is profoundly limited. That choice is not an action in the normal sense—it's not something you do, but an expression of your being.

This, too, is a book that anyone who is serious about leadership will have to read. *Synchronicity* builds directly on Greenleaf's thinking and goes further, especially in illuminating the nature of the choice to lead and the deep understanding or world view out of which such a choice might arise.

For Greenleaf, being a leader has to do with the relationship between the leader and the led. *Only* when the choice to serve undergirds the moral formation of leaders does the hierarchical power that separates the leader and those led not corrupt. Hierarchies are not inherently bad, despite the bad press they receive today.

The potential of hierarchy to corrupt would be dissolved, according to Greenleaf, if leaders chose to serve those they led—if they saw their job, their fundamental reason for being, as true service. For this idea we owe Greenleaf a great debt. His insights also go a long way toward explaining the "leaderlessness" of most contemporary institutions, guided as they are by people who have risen to positions of authority because of technical or decision-making skills, political savvy, or desire for wealth and power.

Joe Jaworski takes Greenleaf's understanding further. He suggests that the fundamental choice that enables true leadership in all situations (including, but not limited to, hierarchical leadership) is the *choice to serve life*. He suggests that in a deep sense, my capacity as a leader comes from my choice to allow life to unfold through me. This choice results in a type of leadership that we've known very rarely, or that we associate exclusively with extraordinary individuals like Gandhi or King. In fact, this domain of leadership is available to us all, and may indeed be crucial for our future.

I believe this broadening of Greenleaf's original insight is so relevant today for two reasons. First, Joe's book shifts the conversation beyond formal power hierarchies of "leaders" and "those led." Increasingly, hierarchies are weakening, and institutions of all sorts, from multinational corporations to school systems, work through informal networks and self-managed teams that form, operate, dissolve, and re-form. It is not enough simply to choose to serve those you are formally leading, because you may not have any formal subordinates in the new organizational structures. Second, Joe's book redirects our attention toward how we collectively shape our destiny.

In the West we tend to think of leadership as a quality that exists in certain people. This usual way of thinking has many traps. We search for special individuals with leadership potential, rather than developing the leadership potential in everyone. We are easily distracted by what this or that leader is doing, by the melodrama of people in power trying to maintain their power and others trying to wrest it from them. When things are going poorly, we blame the situation on incompetent leaders, thereby avoiding any personal responsibility. When things become desperate, we can easily find ourselves waiting for a great leader to rescue us. Through all of this, we totally miss the bigger question: "What are we, collectively, able to create?"

Because of our obsessions with how leaders behave and with the interactions of leaders and followers, we forget that in its essence, leadership is about learning how to shape the future. Leadership exists when people are no longer victims of circumstances but participate in creating new circumstances. When people operate in this domain of generative leadership, day by day, they come to a deepening understanding of, as Joe says, "how the universe actually works." That is the real gift of leadership. It's not about positional power; it's not about accomplishments; it's ultimately not even about what we do. Leadership is about creating a domain in which human beings continually deepen their understanding of reality and become more capable of participating in the unfolding of the world. Ultimately, leadership is about creating new realities.

Exploring such a view of leadership through a book is almost a contradiction in terms. Because this territory can't be fully understood conceptually, any attempt to digest and explain it intellectually is at best a type of map. And the map is not the territory. To understand the territory, we must earn the understanding, and this understanding doesn't come cheaply. We all earn it in our life experience. I think this is one part of what Buddhists mean by "life is suffering." We have to suffer through life, not in the sense of pain, but in terms of living through it.

One way "to live into" these subtle territories of leadership is through a story. When Greenleaf wrote *Servant Leadership*, he "entered" through Hermann Hesse's *Journey to the East*, an autobiographical account of one man's journey in search of enlightenment. Along the way, the narrator's loyal servant, Leo, sustains him through many trials. Years later, when the man finds the esoteric society he is seeking, he discovers that Leo is its leader—so the servant is the leader, and leadership is exercised through service.

Here also Joe enters through a story: his own. The result is an unusual book—rare among leadership books and rare among business books—a personal, reflective account of one person's journey. This may present some difficulties for readers used to "expert" accounts of leadership which give advice and propound theories. Yet Joe's insights about leadership and the process by which he came to those insights are inseparable. His life has been his vehicle for learning, just as his learning has been about how leaders must serve life.

Furthermore, this is not just Joe's story, for Joe's personal story is interwoven with epochal events in which we all participated. This story begins when his father, Leon

Jaworski, became the Watergate Special Prosecutor. During the investigation, Colonel Jaworski became deeply disturbed by the growing evidence implicating Nixon and his closest aides in the Watergate conspiracy. The only person he felt he could talk to without fear of compromising the investigation was his son Joe, also a lawyer. Father and son asked each other the same questions the nation would soon ask: How could this have happened? How could we have come to this—our highest and most trusted officials acting like common criminals?

Living with these questions eventually led Joe to a remarkable series of undertakings. After several years of wrestling with his calling, he decided to leave the prestigious international law firm he had helped build. He struck off into completely foreign territory—public leadership—and created the American Leadership Forum (ALF). The vision of ALF was to establish a national network of talented and diverse midcareer professionals committed to bringing forth a new generation of public leadership. Today, ALF programs operate in a number of communities and regions in the United States with successful results. After almost ten years, Joe stepped down as Chairman of ALF and accepted the position as head of the scenario planning process for the Royal Dutch Shell Group of companies. In this job, he helped shape what many regard as the premier planning process of any large corporation.

For me, Joe's story represents one person's journey taken on behalf of all of us who are wrestling with the profound changes required in public and institutional leadership for the twenty-first century. Our lifelong experiences with hierarchy cast a long shadow, making it difficult for us to think outside the framework of hierarchical leadership. Abuses of hierarchical authority like Watergate, sadly, are still with us today, eliciting deep concerns about our collective capability to lead ourselves. The ALF saga shows what a small group of committed people can do to positively affect public leadership.

Especially interesting for me is the juxtaposition of the ALF and Shell experiences. Joe's years at Shell provide a unique inside look at how Shell's planning process operates, including the first public presentation of the two long-term global scenarios that are now guiding thinking among Shell managers worldwide. Large multinational corporations like Shell represent a new form of social system in the world, with immense power, for good or ill, to influence the future. Today, the global corporation transcends national boundaries and has an impact in the world that goes beyond even that of governments. In this book, we begin to get a glimpse of how this power might positively influence the future. In particular, we see how the scenario process can nurture creative new ways of thinking about and influencing the future both within and beyond the corporation itself.

MEETINGS WITH REMARKABLE PEOPLE

My contact with this book also begins with a story. It was autumn, 1992, and I was in London on the way home from a European trip. I was meeting Joe for breakfast, having not seen him for some five years. In the meantime, he had left ALF, where I had helped in the early start-up period from 1980 to 1983, and he had already been working for Shell for two years. Coincidentally, I had known two of his predecessors in the position, Pierre Wack and Peter Schwartz, as well as Arie de Geus, the former head of all planning for Shell, and had some idea of the extraordinary nature of the job Joe now held. So I was eager to see my old friend and get caught up on his activities.

As he told me about the exciting work of developing Shell's new global scenarios, I became increasingly engaged. Then he told me about the book he was writing. In many ways Joe is a shy person, so writing a book about his life does not come easily. Yet he felt his story contained important lessons that could be shared only through a book. On the one hand, there were the fascinating stories of ALF, and now Shell. But on the other, below the surface detail of these activities, were the profound personal changes Joe had gone through, guided by a series of meetings with remarkable people such as John Gardner, Harlan Cleveland, and some of the leading scientists of our time. I was stunned when Joe told me about meeting the physicist David Bohm in 1980, a meeting I had never known about. As time had passed, Joe had come to realize that this meeting was pivotal, and that the conversation with Bohm had planted seeds within him that had taken years to develop and that now were leading him to a radically new view of how human beings could shape their destiny. When our breakfast ended, I told Joe I would do anything I could to help him finish this book.

I, too, had had a pivotal meeting with David Bohm. It was in 1989, as I was in the very final stages of writing *The Fifth Discipline*. David gave a small seminar at

MIT for a group of us interested in his work on dialogue. At the time, I was searching desperately for a deeper theoretical understanding of a particular phenomenon I had observed in teams, which I felt was essential to understand the discipline of team learning. Over the years my colleagues and I had come to use the term "alignment" to describe what happens when people in a group actually start to function as a whole. We would use examples like extraordinary jazz ensembles and championship basketball teams to evoke a sense of what alignment was all about. But I knew at a deeper level I could not begin to explain how this mysterious functioning as a whole actually came about.

I also knew that what I was looking for was not available in mainstream contemporary management theories about teams. Many of these theories are essentially individualistic in nature, grounded in individual psychology or the psychology of groups. I felt deeply that this phenomenon of alignment was not individualistic at all, but fundamentally collective. I knew of no theory that in any way started to explain how the seemingly mysterious state of "being in the groove" (as the jazz musicians call it) or "in the zone" actually works. Theories based on individual reasoning, interpersonal interactions, or behavior patterns in groups seemed inherently inadequate.

In the seminar, as Bohm described his work on dialogue, I said to myself, "At least now I know I'm not crazy." Bohm talked about the phenomenon of thought and how our patterns of thought can hold us captive. "Thought creates the world and then says 'I didn't do it,'" he said. He talked about a "generative order" in which, depending on our state of consciousness, we "participate in how reality unfolds." Bohm's theory went beyond interdependence to wholeness. Interdependence is something you can see. For example, a mother and a child are interdependent in countless ways you can observe. Such interdependence is a sort of window into a deeper domain of wholeness. Interdependence exists at what Bohm called the "explicate" level. But wholeness exists at the "implicate," which is the unmanifest or premanifest level. When we are engaged in something that is deeply meaningful and are attuned to one another, human beings can participate in the "unfolding" of the implicate wholeness into the manifest or explicate order.

Now, this conversation in 1989 with David Bohm was a sort of seed planting for me as well. I knew I only dimly grasped what Bohm was saying, parts of which resonated deeply with me. Other parts seemed strange, foreign to any way I had been trained to think. Over the years, reading and rereading *Wholeness and the Implicate Order*, where Bohm lays out the basic theory, had helped. But when Joe started to tell me that morning about his conversation with Bohm, I realized that here was a very special gift. Later, when Joe showed me the transcript of the conversation (he somehow had had the presence of mind to tape the meeting), I was struck by the simplicity and clarity of Bohm's way of explaining his thinking to Joe. In many ways, the personal nature of Joe's questions seemed to allow David to speak personally as well. Having studied his work, I can say that there are subtleties to David's thinking that I only began to understand through Joe's meeting with him. I realized that, in a sense, Joe and the story he was and is living out had the potential to become a vehicle for communicating David's seminal insights to a much bigger audience than he would ever reach with his own writings.

Perhaps in some way David and the other leading thinkers with whom Joe met sensed this as well. Otherwise, it is hard to understand how these meetings even would have occurred. By the time Joe met him in 1980, Bohm was already a famous physicist. Einstein had once said that Bohm was the one person from whom he ever understood quantum theory. Bohm had written the leading textbook on quantum theory in the early 1950s. Why would this man, who was quite reserved and protective of his privacy, agree, on one day's notice, to spend the next afternoon with a strange American lawyer who had just called him on the telephone?

The answer lies in part in Joe's personal qualities, which somehow make it possible for people to open up to him. Joe has less investment in appearing to understand things than almost anybody I know. He'll often say, "You know, I don't think I really understand it," or, "I'm not sure if I'm doing it justice." To have accomplished what he's accomplished, and to have the kind of fame that he inherited from his father, and still to have retained that childlike quality of being able to wonder, is really extraordinary. I've never met anybody who's as good at wondering as Joe is. Perhaps this is one reason people are so open around him.

Another less obvious reason is that people like Bohm probably had a sense that it was important to talk to Joe. They felt they should spend time with him. There is a sense of destiny that travels with Joe. It's a very subtle phenomenon to describe because many people have lofty goals, and many people have a sense of self-importance. Joe has absolutely none of that. The sense of destiny I experience around Joe is actually *around* him, not *in* him. It's not in his personality. If Joe says,

"This is really important," it's because that's the reality he's seeing, not because he's expressing an opinion. Little of him blocks what's going on around him.

I've come to appreciate that one of the gifts of artists is the ability to see the world as it really is. The vision of what painters or sculptors intend to create is critical, but it is of little use if they cannot accurately observe the current state of their creation. Most of us aren't very good at perceiving reality as it is. Most of what we "see" is shaped by our impressions, our history, our baggage, our preconceptions. We can't see people as they really are because we're too busy reacting to our own internal experiences of what they evoke in us, so we rarely actually relate to reality. We mostly relate to internal remembrances of our own history, stimulated and evoked by whatever is externally before us.

Somehow Joe has a more direct relationship with things than most of us, and I think this is what sensitive people see in him. It's not just that Joe is a good listener, or a good questioner, or a childlike learner. I think people such as David Bohm have the feeling that by telling Joe their story, their story will actually be *heard*. A type of fidelity emerges from this. Joe tells his story, but our experience of it is much more like looking through a window than watching a movie. We don't just hear his memories, we look through his experiences at something that was actually there. And when we can see what is true, something new can show up. I think this is why people like David Bohm and the biologist Francisco Varela, who have come to understand what it means to operate clearly in the moment, believe they must spend time with this person.

I share these impressions of how Joe works not to flatter him but, I hope, to help you appreciate at a more personal level what this story is all about. If we could only see reality more as it is, it would become obvious what we need to do. We wouldn't be acting out of our own histories, or our own needs, or our own purely reactive interpretations. We would see what is needed in the moment. We would do exactly what's required of us, right now, right here. This is precisely what David Bohm was talking about when he spoke of living one's life by "participating in the unfolding." You can't do that unless you can actually see what is right before you. In this way, Joe's story is a beautiful demonstration of the personal orientation required for a learning organization to operate.

Moving as it does between historic public events and key intellectual developments, Joe's story naturally draws us in. We are all seeking greater insight into these remarkable times, when there is so much cause for both despair and hope. Even though our political and institutional leadership is losing respect and credibility, and core societal crises fester, we are gaining a greater understanding of how the universe works. An historic shift in the Western scientific-materialistic world view is occurring. Perhaps the two are connected. Perhaps our institutions and leadership are, by and large, grounded in a way of thinking about the world that is increasingly obsolete and counterproductive. Perhaps that is why they are falling apart.

The new leadership must be grounded in fundamentally new understandings of how the world works. The sixteenth-century Newtonian mechanical view of the universe, which still guides our thinking, has become increasingly dysfunctional in these times of interdependence and change. The critical shifts required to guarantee a healthy world for our children and our children's children will not be achieved by doing more of the same. "The world we have created is a product of our way of thinking," said Einstein. Nothing will change in the future without fundamentally new ways of thinking. This is the real work of leadership. And this book is a good place to begin the work.

FUNDAMENTAL SHIFTS OF MIND

As the book was nearing completion, the story implicit in Joe's experiences began to emerge with so much coherence that it seemed to just tell itself. Through a series of working sessions with Joe and Betty Sue Flowers, Joe's editor, we'd find, again and again, whenever something was unclear, we'd simply ask Joe, "Well, tell us what actually happened," and he would. As we listened, we'd shake our heads and say, "Well, just write it that way." Eventually, the whole process began to resemble a sort of personal archeology as Betty Sue and I would simply guide Joe in sharing his first-hand experience.

Then I began to feel that we needed to step back from the story and reflect more broadly on the whole journey. At one level, the larger purpose of the book was to suggest that we can shape our future in ways that we rarely realize. What made Joe's story so compelling was that it offered an emerging understanding of how this might come about.

One afternoon I asked Joe, "What are the guiding principles, or the organizing principles, with which this book is concerned?" Almost without hesitation, he responded by describing certain necessary shifts of mind and the consequences of these shifts. He acknowledged that this was all very new to him and that these ideas should be treated as preliminary insights, initial glimpses into a vast new territory. Nonetheless, I think they will be helpful, especially for those readers who would like a conceptual road map before embarking on Joe's journey.

First, Joe said, we need to be open to *fundamental shifts of mind*. We have very deep mental models of how the world works, deeper than we can know. To think that the world can ever change without changes in our mental models is folly. When I asked Joe more specifically what these changes might be about, he said that *it's about a shift from seeing a world made up of things to seeing a world that's open and primarily made up of relationships*, where whatever is manifest, whatever we see, touch, feel, taste, and hear, whatever seems most real to us, is actually nonsubstantial. A deeper level of reality exists beyond anything we can articulate.

Once we understand this, we begin to see that the future is not fixed, that *we live in a world of possibilities*. And yet almost all of us carry around a deep sense of resignation. We're resigned to believing we can't have any influence in the world, at least not on a scale that matters. So we focus on the small scale, where we think we can have an influence. We do our best with our kids, or we work on our relationships, or we focus on building a career. But deep down, we're resigned to being absolutely powerless in the larger world. Yet if we have a world of people who all feel powerless, we have a future that's predetermined. So we live in hopelessness and helplessness, a state of great despair. And this despair is actually a product of how we think, a kind of self-fulfilling prophecy.

For the most part, this despair is undiscussable, especially among successful people. We don't want to talk about it, because we want to maintain a facade of having our lives together. So we create all kinds of diversions. Our culture itself offers abundant diversions. It tells us that all we need to worry about is how we look. Work out, get the body in shape, dress well. Life is about appearances. Diversions also exist in the story we tell about the world—that the world is dominated by politics and self-interest, for example. All these diversions are simply ways of covering up the deeper sense of despair arising from our feeling that we can do nothing about the future.

But when we go through this shift of mind, we begin to realize that the sense of despair we've been feeling arises out of a fundamentally naive view of the world. In fact, absolutely everything around us is in continual motion. There's nothing in nature that stays put. When I look at the leaves on the tree, I am really seeing a flowing of life. Those leaves won't be on that tree in a couple of months. At this very moment, they're changing. Before long, they'll be a different color. Before long, they'll be lying on the ground. Before long, they'll be part of the soil. Before long, they'll be part of another tree. There's absolutely nothing in nature that stays put.

One of the great mysteries of our current state of consciousness is how we can live in a world where absolutely nothing is fixed, and yet perceive a world of "fixedness." But once we start to see reality more as it is, we realize that nothing is permanent, so how could the future be fixed? How could we live in anything but a world of continual possibility? This realization allows us to feel more alive. People like David Bohm and the management expert W. Edwards Deming had just such vitality. Where did they get it? Perhaps they had less of their consciousness tied up in maintaining the illusion of fixity, so they had a little more life left in them. Because of how we think, we're strangling the life out of ourselves. When we start to see the world more as it is, we stop strangling ourselves.

That afternoon when we talked, Joe said, *"When this fundamental shift of mind occurs, our sense of identity shifts, too,* and we *begin to accept each other as legitimate human beings."* I've only just now reached a point in my life where I can begin to appreciate what it would actually mean to accept one another as legitimate human beings. Part of that ironclad grip on ourselves which maintains the illusion of fixity involves seeing our own selves and each other as fixed. I don't see you; I see the stored-up images, interpretations, feelings, doubts, distrusts, likes, and dislikes that you evoke in me. When we actually begin to accept one another as legitimate human beings, it's truly amazing.

Perhaps this is what love means. Virtually all the world's religions have, in one way or another, recognized the power of love, this quality of seeing one another as legitimate human beings.

"Then," Joe said, "when *we start to accept this fundamental shift of mind, we begin to see ourselves as part of the unfolding. We also see that it's actually impossible for our lives not to have meaning."* The only way I can experience my life as meaningless is to work as hard as I possibly can to tell myself it has no meaning. At a deeper level of reality, my life can't help but have meaning, because everything is continually unfolding, and I am connected into that unfolding in ways that I can't even imagine. It takes no effort of will, no particular skill, no learning, no knowledge. It is actually my birthright. It's what it means to be alive. Robert Frost said that home is that place you shouldn't have to earn. We don't have to earn this type of meaningfulness in our lives. It is already present.

Joe said, *"Operating in this different state of mind and being, we come to a very different sense of what it means to be committed."* In our traditional image of commitment, things get done by hard work. We have to sacrifice. If everything starts to fall apart, we try harder, or we tell ourselves that we're not good enough, or that we don't care enough to be that committed. So we vacillate between two states of being, one a form of self-manipulation, wherein we get things done by telling ourselves that if we don't work harder, it won't get done; and the other a state of guilt, wherein we say we're not good enough. Neither of these states of being has anything to do with the deeper nature of commitment.

When we operate in the state of mind in which we realize we are part of the unfolding, we can't *not* be committed. It's actually impossible not to be committed. Nothing ever happens by accident. Every single thing is part of what needs to happen right now. We only make the mistakes that we have to make to learn what we're here to learn right now. This is a commitment of being, not a commitment of doing. We discover that our being is inherently in a state of commitment as part of the unfolding process. The only way to be uncommitted is to lose that realization, to once again fall into the illusion that we aren't participating in life. This discovery leads to a paradoxical *integrity of surrender*, surrendering into commitment: I actualize my commitment by listening, out of which my "doing" arises. Sometimes the greatest acts of commitment involve doing nothing but sitting and waiting until I just know what to do next.

In most of our organizations today, managers who adopt this attitude would be considered nonmanagers because they are not doing anything to fix problems. We're hooked on the notion that commitment and activity are inseparable. So we create a continual stream of activity, making sure that everybody sees us doing lots of things so they'll believe we're actually committed. If we stay busy enough, maybe we'll even convince ourselves that our lives have some meaning even though, deep down, we know they couldn't possibly have any meaning, because everything is hopeless, and we're helpless, and we couldn't possibly affect anything anyhow.

One of the interesting indicators of this paradoxical connection between our sense of helplessness and our ceaseless activity is how much difficulty we have actually saying, "You know, I can't do anything about that." We often find that people in organizations have to create a belief that they can make change happen in order to justify their meaningless activity. So they're caught in an enormous set of contradictions. At one level, they believe they can't influence anything. At another level, they create a story that says, "We can make it happen," and they busy themselves doing things that they know won't have any impact. It's like rats on a treadmill; they get tired after a while. Recently a very successful manager told me that she had suddenly realized that all her life she had just been treading water. We live in a contradictory state of frenzied commitment, of treading water, knowing we're actually not going any place. But we're terrified that if we stop, we'll drown. Our lives will be meaningless.

When this new type of commitment starts to operate, there is a flow around us. Things just seem to happen. We begin to see that with very small movements, at just the right time and place, all sorts of consequent actions are brought into being. We develop what artists refer to as an "economy of means," where, rather than getting things done through effort and brute force, we start to operate very subtly. A flow of meaning begins to operate around us, as if we were part of a larger conversation. This is the ancient meaning of dialogue: (*dia • logos*) "flow of meaning." We start to notice that things suddenly are just attracted to us in ways that are very puzzling. A structure of underlying causes, a set of forces, begins to operate, as if we were surrounded by a magnetic field with magnets being aligned spontaneously in this field. But this alignment is not spontaneous at all—it's just that the magnets are responding to a more subtle level of causality.

When we started the MIT Center for Organizational Learning a few years ago, a most remarkable thing began to happen. People just started showing up. In one period of about two or three months, three incredible women showed up. I had met them eleven years before at a particular meeting, and I had begun to think about them again because the work they were doing connected in important ways to new developments at the Center. But I didn't know how to reach any of them, or even where they lived. Within two months, each of them had called and said she had learned about what we were doing and wanted to see how she could help.

The causes of such incidents are very hard for us to understand, but it appears that when we start to operate in this new state of mind, grounded in this different commitment, something starts to operate around us. You could call it "attraction"— the attractiveness of people in a state of surrender.

Lastly, *when we are in a state of commitment and surrender, we begin to experience what is sometimes called "synchronicity."* In other words, synchronicity is a result. It's important to understand the underlying causes of synchronicity, because if we don't, we might actually try to bring about synchronicity in the same way we try to control the rest of our lives. People tend to elevate synchronicity into a sort of magical, mystical experience. In fact, it's very down to earth. Water flows downhill because of gravity. Of course, gravity itself is a pretty mysterious phenomenon. It seems to be a type of field, as if all physical objects in the universe have some attraction for one another. But even though no one knows exactly how gravity works, we can observe the result: water flows downhill. We don't argue about the result because it is observable. That's much the way synchronicity seems to operate in this field of deep commitment.

In the same sense, this attractiveness, the field that starts to develop around people who have experienced these shifts of mind, creates a phenomenon that Joe calls predictable miracles. "Miracle" is a funny word because it connotes the unusual or mysterious. But in fact, what is "miraculous" might be just what is beyond our current understanding and way of living. If we were not making such an immense effort to separate ourselves from life, we might actually live life day to day, minute by minute, as a series of predictable miracles.

PART ONE

PREPARING TO JOURNEY

><+>—o—<+><

WHATEVER YOU CAN DO, OR DREAM YOU CAN, BEGIN IT.

BOLDNESS HAS GENIUS, POWER, AND MAGIC IN IT.

—Goethe

1. WATERGATE

It was October 1973, and I was thirty-nine years old. Watergate had broken out in September of the previous year. I was in the midst of living "the good life," and although I had been following the news accounts of the Watergate affair fairly closely, it was more background noise than anything else. My attention was focused on practicing law in Houston, Texas, building an international law firm, and managing my business affairs.

The Senate Watergate Committee was in full operation, and John Dean, the President's counsel, had testified that President Nixon knew of the Watergate cover-up as early as September 1972. There was also testimony that John Ehrlichman, one of the President's closest advisors, had approved cash payments to the Watergate burglars. The Committee had heard testimony to the effect that the President had installed a voice-activated taping system in the Oval Office, which had recorded all conversations taking place there without the visitor's knowledge or consent.

Nixon's two closest associates, Ehrlichman and H. R. Haldeman, had resigned. John Dean had been fired. Archibald Cox, the Watergate Special Prosecutor, had subpoenaed tape recordings from the White House that were relevant to the case, and subsequently was fired as Special Prosecutor on orders from President Nixon. Attorney General Elliot Richardson, who had selected Cox for the job, refused to comply with Nixon's orders and resigned. His deputy, William Ruckelshaus, likewise refused to fire Cox, and was discharged. Solicitor General Robert Bork, next in the line of succession, was appointed acting Attorney General and removed Cox from office.

This series of events was dubbed by the press as the "Saturday Night Massacre." By this time, like most Americans, I had become deeply alarmed, and I felt that there must be much more to this than had already surfaced.

In late October, General Alexander Haig, Nixon's Chief of Staff, telephoned my father, Leon Jaworski, and said he wanted to discuss his taking the Special Prosecutor's job. My father flew to Washington the next morning. Public reaction to the Saturday Night Massacre apparently had been much more violent than the White House had anticipated. Congress was considering creating a separate Special Prosecutor's Office outside the President's control.

In that meeting, Haig urged my father to take the job. "The situation in this country is almost revolutionary. Things are about to come apart. The only hope of stabilizing the situation is for the President to be able to announce that someone in whom the country has confidence has agreed to serve." My father agreed to take the job only if he was assured that he would be able to pursue the investigation with complete independence, and that he would have the right to take the President to court if necessary.

During the following months, my father was to discover the frightening dimensions of the Watergate conspiracy, and he was to share those with me, in confidence, as he learned of them. This was a life-changing experience for me.

>–•–O–•–<

It was Halloween night when my father returned home from the meeting with General Haig. News of his acceptance had leaked out in Washington, so media representatives had assembled at the house. Most members of our family had gathered there, and the air felt electric with excitement.

But later that night, I went for a long walk alone. I thought of the sacrifice my father was about to make. He was sixty-eight years old, in the process of retiring. I worried about his health, and the enormous stress he would be experiencing in the coming months. Most people knew him as a member of the establishment, the senior partner of one of the most powerful law firms in the country, and one of the best litigators in the United States.

I knew him quite differently. I knew him as the son of a Polish immigrant and as a rare and great American—a modest, almost self-conscious man, who held a deep belief that when we are called, we must serve. He abhorred being in the limelight. In the midst of pressure and controversy, he sought simple pleasures, working close to the earth, spending a lot of time gardening. He raised beautiful azaleas and camellias which he loved to photograph.

When I was young, every evening I would ride my bicycle to the bus stop to meet my father, and then we would walk back home together to our big white house. Many times after dinner, he would take the car and go back to the office, particularly when he was in trial, which seemed to be almost all the time. But there was plenty of time for the children: playing in the parks together, tossing the baseball on weekends, playing at the beach, fishing. On Sunday mornings, he would put all three of us on his lap and read the funny papers to us. He was a wonderful father. Then World War II came and it all changed.

One afternoon, I was playing outside when all of a sudden my father showed up. It was much earlier than he normally came home. I followed him into the house where my mother was polishing furniture and doing some general housework. She looked up and said, "Well, Mr. Jaworski, what are you doing home this time of day?"

And my father replied, "Captain Jaworski to you, my dear." I remember the look of dismay on my mother's face. From that moment on, our lives would never be the same.

We didn't see much of our father after that. While he was overseas, it was really rough on my mother. She would wait for his letters, and when they came, we would all crowd around her in the living room. We would stand very close to our mother while she would try to read the letters to us without crying. She never made it. We would all clutch her and hold her tight while she was crying, sometimes uncontrollably, as she read.

When my father came back from Europe, he was an altogether different person. We went to the train station to meet him, and the first thing I noticed was that he was chain-smoking cigarettes. He hadn't smoked cigarettes before. When we got home, what I remember more clearly than anything else over the next few days was that he was cursing: "damn" and "hell" and "son of a bitch." I'd never heard him use those words before. There was an edge to him, a harshness. He didn't care much about the flowers. He seemed nervous and began working very hard almost immediately.

Later, when I was older, he told me that many of his friends and partners had stayed home and not gone to the war. They had made a lot of money in the meantime, while we were in pretty pressed financial shape because of his war-time pay. He had a lot of catching up to do, so he began dedicating himself to that. It was pretty much that way from then on for as long as I can remember. All of his partners and young associates at the firm referred to him as "the Colonel," and I began doing so also. As I look back at it, this seemed to mark the change in our relationship.

During the first week when he was back, he insisted that I take boxing lessons. I didn't want to take boxing lessons, and when I told him so, he shamed me for being afraid. He seemed to be very disappointed in me, which hurt. This was the first of a series of events that reflected the kind of relationship I had with the Colonel from that point forward. I was an unself-conscious, silly, but sensitive and vulnerable boy, full of wonder and imagination and open to all possibilities. I was always trying to get his attention, trying to get him to accept me for what I was and what I wanted to be. It was a struggle that lasted for years and years. In the long run, I became fiercely independent, and so opposed to anyone controlling me that I think I went overboard with it.

Maybe that's why for years I was so wild. Even before the fifth grade, I was always organizing mischief. I would get my older sister to help me put big rocks on the railroad track to see what would happen. Another time, I set fire to a field, not intentionally, but I was playing with fire. The fire could have burned up a whole block of houses if the fire department hadn't handled it promptly. When I was in fourth grade, I found some mules grazing in a field, and I thought it would really be funny to turn them loose in my school building, so I did. At thirteen, I would sneak out of the house and roll the Colonel's car down the driveway, very quietly, and then go out driving for a couple of hours, coming back just before daybreak, when the Colonel would get up and go to work. At sixteen, I took his pickup truck and drove to Mexico for a week with a couple of my buddies.

►─◆►─○─◄◆─┤◄

When my father went to Washington to take over the job as the Watergate Prosecutor, he didn't know whom in his office he could really trust. Those early months were tough on him. He was known as the President's man, the lawyer who supposedly could be controlled, the friend of Lyndon Johnson, who knew where power lay and respected it. His staff of seventy-five was composed of young lawyers who were mostly inherited from Cox. My father was hampered by the disaffection of some members of that staff, and like most people under those circumstances, felt a certain degree of self-doubt. We talked over the telephone often during those early days.

In a telephone call just before Christmas, the Colonel's voice was grave. He said he could not talk about things over the telephone, but he wondered if I would be at the family ranch when he could spend a few days there over Christmas.

Our ranch lay between the little village of Wimberly and Austin, Texas, on Ranch Road 12. The Colonel had bought the land in the late 1940s, after he came back from the war, and had paid thirty dollars an acre for it. It was solid cedar and scrub. For those first five years, from the age of fourteen through eighteen, I worked summers and most holidays with the crews who were clearing that land. The Colonel would often join us, and he got tremendous satisfaction out of creating parklike settings from areas so densely covered with scrub and cedar that not even grass could grow. In later years, it became a family affair, almost a ritual, where the Colonel, my brother-in-law, and I would spend weekends at the ranch, getting up early, before the heat became unbearable, to chop cedar, pull dead stumps, and burn the scrub. This was the Colonel's sacred place, where he cleared his mind, and where he got his energy.

>┼◆┼─◦─◆┼◄

After receiving the Colonel's telephone call, I arranged to take a couple of days off to spend at the ranch. On the way up, I thought about how serious he had sounded over the telephone. I was anxious to hear about the developments in Washington over the previous few weeks.

When I got there that evening, the Colonel seemed tired, and we spent the time after dinner just catching up on things in general and talking over the business of the quarter-horse operation at the ranch.

After breakfast the next morning, we loaded up the Jeep with all the necessary paraphernalia—chainsaws, double-edged axes, pickaxes, plenty of cold water, fruit, and a few beers. At about seven-thirty, we struck out for the "boondocks," as the Colonel called it, and went to work. We cleared cedar without stopping for a couple of hours, and when we took a long break, the Colonel and I sat under a big oak and talked.

It was the same as it had been for twenty years. He always wore the same clothes up there. As my mother put it, "He looked like something the cat drug in." His baggy pants were stuffed into his Red Wing work boots and held up by a belt that had seen its better days years before. His shirt was a khaki army shirt from his war years, which had the sleeves cut out of it. After working for a few hours, the clothes were soaked with sweat, and there were wood chips, grime, and dirt throughout his hair and eyebrows. As I think about it, I smile. His face looked like a chimney sweep's. But that's when he was the most relaxed, the happiest.

As we squatted down under the tree, the Colonel began to tell me what was on his mind. "Bud, we've been listening to the tapes. The President is up to his ears in this thing. I heard the President of the United States, a lawyer who took the same oath that you and I took, suborning perjury like a common criminal. He was telling Haldeman how to testify under oath untruthfully and yet sidestep perjury. Here is the President of the United States, his counsel, and his Chief of Staff—three of the most powerful men in the country, people charged with the highest responsibility in our government—and I heard them talking and plotting against the ends of justice like thugs. Sleazy, third-rate criminals." His voice was rising, and his eyes were flashing. He got up, went to the Jeep, and pulled out a brown cardboard envelope, which he almost threw down at my feet. "Here—just take a look at this!"

We began leafing through the transcript. The part the Colonel had referred to was the now infamous March 21, 1973, conversation among Nixon, Dean, and Haldeman, and, as my father had told me, contained the portion in which Nixon was coaching Haldeman on how to lie under oath without committing perjury. Their language was a mixture of disjointed phrases, profanities, and obscenities. It was like two guys half-drunk in a back room shooting craps. They talked about getting a million dollars to pay in blackmail money to keep things quiet. What was contained in this transcript was clearly sufficient in my mind to permit a jury to conclude beyond a reasonable doubt that the President had joined a conspiracy. It was clear that Nixon was up to his eyeballs in the entire business.

My mind flashed back to the many times I had heard Nixon speak to the American people on television about Watergate, reassuring us that he was not involved, that this whole affair was blown out of proportion. That was the public Nixon. Now I was seeing the private Nixon—the real Richard Nixon. His betrayal of the Constitution and his staggering abuse of power made me sick to my stomach. Revulsion and hate welled up in me. I had a feeling of fear for our entire country, fear that followed the realization that we were being led by a man with so little character. How could someone with such a low moral and ethical base ascend to the highest office of the most powerful nation in the world? How could this happen? Who was responsible? How could we prevent this from ever happening again?

I looked at the Colonel, and I could see that his heart and his soul were aching like mine. He was looking down at the ground, scratching in the dirt with a twig, and then he looked up at me and said, "When I went up there, I never ever expected to find the President in the middle of this. It never even occurred to me that he was in the driver's seat. The situation is explosive. But you can't breathe a word of this to anyone. It would prejudice the right of others, and eventually Nixon himself, to a fair trial."

I knew this without the Colonel even saying so. I knew he badly needed someone just to confide in—someone whom he trusted, with whom he could share this. He talked of a deep premonition that things were going to get much worse than anyone in Washington ever imagined. And it was on his shoulders to help see the nation through one of the most traumatic events in its history. I reassured him. "Colonel, stay after it. I know you'll continue to do the right thing."

"With God's help," he added.

The hardest thing for me in the weeks and months that followed was to have this knowledge and, at the same time, watch the President lie to the American people on television. It's impossible to describe the feeling of contempt I had as I watched him. I was disillusioned with our political leadership, but I recognized that we all bore some personal responsibility for what was happening in Washington. We were getting what we deserved. I began thinking about the role that ordinary citizens like myself should be playing in the life of our country.

About a month after I met with the Colonel, the Attorney General and his six codefendants appeared in Judge Sirica's court for their arraignment on the Watergate cover-up indictment. They were all charged with one count of conspiracy to obstruct justice. In the Colonel's words, it was "an unparalleled American tragedy . . . an historic moment." There stood the former chief law enforcement officer in the country, the former Assistant to the President, the Special Counsel to the President, an official of the Committee to Re-Elect the President, and the General Counsel to the United States Information Agency. All but one were lawyers—a painful fact, which the Colonel and I talked about many times.

Over the next several months, the Colonel's staff, the media, and the public gained more confidence in him. Talk of Congress appointing its own Special Prosecutor subsided. Sixty-four additional tapes were subpoenaed, including the tape of June 23, 1972, which proved beyond a shadow of a doubt that not only the Presidential aides, but the President himself had participated in the Watergate cover-up. I was there in July when the Colonel and his team argued their case before the Supreme Court of the United States. Within three weeks, the Court handed down its decision confirming that the "charter" the President had given him as Special Prosecutor did in fact guarantee him the right and the power to take anyone, including the President, to court; that this charter had the effect of law; and that the Supreme Court was the final authority on the law. The Court's decision was unanimous, and it confirmed that the President, who had been named an unindicted coconspirator in the Watergate cases, had to produce the sixty-four tapes of Watergate conversations. Nixon had tried to get away with turning over a few edited summaries and garbled transcriptions of the tapes, which, as it turned out, were incomplete and riddled with errors.

Within a few weeks, the Colonel had these tapes, which included some conversations between the President and Haldeman on June 23, just six days after the Watergate break-in. On that tape, they talked about using the CIA to get the FBI out of the investigation. Neither Haig nor Nixon's Chief Counsel, James St. Clair, had known about that particular tape. St. Clair told Nixon to reveal this publicly or he was going to resign. On the afternoon of August 5, the President released his statement, and admitted that the tapes were "at variance" with his previous statements. Now his own transcript showed that he had known of the cover-up, and participated in it, six days after the break-in.

Of this moment, the Colonel would later write, "For me, the revelation was the end of the nightmare. . . . The conclusions I had reached about [Nixon's] culpability were now confirmed and absolutely clarified. . . . I had walked the streets of Washington knowing that he continually twisted the facts while I, who knew the truth, had to remain silent. The relief I felt is impossible to describe."

Two days later, on August 7, 1974, Nixon resigned. The rest was a mopping-up operation, and by the end of October, the Colonel had resigned and was on his way back to Houston.

▷·┼◁▷·○·◁▷·┼◁

It had been only one year, but what a year it had been. Watergate proved that the American Constitution works, and, as the Colonel put it, "No one—absolutely no one—is above the law." But the events of that year left a profound personal mark on me, as it did on most Americans who lived through that national tragedy. I wondered whether any sitting president would ever be fully trusted again. Further, I saw this as an issue not just of political leadership, but of institutional leadership in general. I began to consider the self-reinforcing problems confronting us: unscrupulous leaders who abuse the power entrusted to them, and lazy, self-indulgent citizens who, in effect, invite this kind of behavior. I felt deep concern and a real sense of personal responsibility about this state of affairs, but what bothered me even more was my own sense of powerlessness to make lasting change. How could we get a handle on this problem and really make a difference?

The seeds were planted for what would amount to a major change in the way I would spend the balance of my life, but it would be years before I developed the capacity to let those seeds grow.

2. MAKING A MARK

By the time Watergate was unfolding, I had been practicing law for thirteen years, and by most standards I had achieved success. I had married my high school sweetheart, Fran, and we were raising a son. We had everything we could ask for: my highly rewarding professional life, a large comfortable home in a beautiful neighborhood, all the material things we wanted, a healthy and well-rounded eleven-year-old son, and lots of friends and close family in Houston.

It was a kind of picture-book life, while it lasted.

▷━◆━○━◆━◁

In the late 1960s, I was one of the leading partners in the law firm, on the Operating Committee, and among the top producers in fees and new client business. In addition to my professional life, I helped start a life insurance company with some of my old fraternity buddies. Years later the company was sold to a nationally recognized financial institution. In the meantime, a group of these same friends and I built one of the first refineries in Alaska. The project was barely completed when a publicly held company purchased it from us. We were on a real roll—it was a high stakes sort of life and financially very rewarding.

But it was practicing law and building the law firm that captured most of my attention. The entrepreneurial process was exhilarating for all of us—the more we succeeded, the harder we'd push. We committed to the best office space and began recruiting the brightest lawyers from the best law schools. For many years, I was responsible for the recruiting process, and I used to dearly love the challenge of competing against the major law firms for the best talent available. Teams of the best lawyers in the firm would fan out across the country on these recruiting trips. It was a highly gratifying experience to meet with these graduating students, tell them our "war stories," and enroll them in our dream. It was a cause for real celebration each time we recruited a star who was highly sought after by one of the premier firms.

By this time, my relationship with the Colonel was better than it had ever been. The larger our law firm grew, and the better our reputation got, the more the Colonel seemed to like it. His pride in my accomplishments was extremely important to me, although I never would acknowledge that to him.

It was not easy growing up in the Colonel's shadow. He was one of the most respected lawyers in the country, at the very pinnacle of the profession. Every time I made an appearance before a court, I was being compared to the lawyer who had begun the practice of law at nineteen and who had never lost a jury case. This was an impossible act to follow. Further, the Colonel was not easily impressed by anyone—you had to earn his respect "the old-fashioned way." He was somewhat reserved, but he had his share of ego. When any of his children received his praise, we tended to remember it.

The Colonel was a member, and later the President, of the American College of Trial Lawyers, the most elite club of trial lawyers in the country. Less than 1 percent of the trial lawyers in the country are admitted to this society. The Colonel and my mother would go to the meetings of the College twice a year, and in the late 1960s, he would occasionally invite Fran and me to go along. He would introduce me to the greatest trial lawyers in the country, and I would sit around with them and listen to their stories. It was an absolutely wonderful experience for me. I learned a lot; these men were like mentors to me, and I aspired to be like them.

At one of the meetings, Robert Clare, a senior partner of Sherman and Sterling, one of Wall Street's most prestigious firms, began telling me of a major lawsuit he had referred to one of the premier firms in Houston. They had come back to him and said there was no way the lawsuit could be won, and that he had better just pack it in and go home. He said he felt awful about this, and that there should be some way that recovery could be made. He asked my opinion about it, describing the case briefly to me. I looked him straight in the eye and said that we could get the kind of results he was looking for. So he sent the case down to us, and we were ultimately highly successful.

As a result, Bob began sending other cases to us, and we enjoyed a wonderful relationship with his firm. In 1976 I was admitted to fellowship in the College and at one of the meetings, Bob, who was one of the Colonel's closet friends, came up to the Colonel and said, "How's the second-best lawyer in the world?" The Colonel looked puzzled and before he could say anything, Bob explained, "Of course, your son is the greatest." Now we all knew that wasn't true, but it was a great way for Bob to pay me the ultimate compliment—and the Colonel just loved it. Every time they came together from then on, Bob would greet the Colonel the same way, and the Colonel would stand there grinning. I felt "seen" by the Colonel for the very first time since he had returned from overseas after the war.

The life of a litigator was fast paced and full of excitement. Fran and I seemed to manage the hectic pace just fine, even in the face of unusual circumstances. When our son Joey was born, I was trying a lawsuit in Federal Court in Houston. When her labor began, Fran never questioned whether I should spend the day with her. "Go on to work," she said, "and I'll let the office know when the baby is ready to arrive, and then you can come to the hospital."

I made arrangements with one of the partners at the firm to keep me advised of Fran's progress. I planned on telling the Court of my situation, assured the judge would adjourn for the day and then I could go over to the hospital. But it didn't quite work out that way because I was in the court of a rather old-fashioned judge. When my partner came over to say that Fran was in intensive labor, I approached the bench, but the judge said, "Well, she can have the baby without you. It's not necessary for you to go. Put on your next witness, counselor." Luckily, I made it to the hospital just as Joey was being delivered.

In 1967, the Colonel and I started a quarter-horse breeding operation on the ranch. We originally conceived this project, "Circle J Enterprises," as a tax shelter, but it soon became highly successful in its own right. I was the managing partner, and we had an absolutely first-rate ranch manager, Royce Baker, who ran the operation on a day-to-day basis. I devoted every available weekend to this undertaking. On Friday afternoons, Fran, Joey, and I would drive up to the ranch from Houston. I would complete my office work in the back seat while Fran drove. We would arrive at the ranch late at night, returning to Houston the following Sunday evening.

As the horse operation grew, we began showing horses around the country. We had purchased a young stud, Magnolia Pay, and successfully campaigned him to become an American Quarter Horse Association supreme champion, one of only sixteen in the world at the time. Magnolia Pay "nicked" beautifully with the brood mare band that we had assembled, and his offspring became highly marketable. Early on, one of the horses we raised was named the world champion halter mare, and the following year we bred the world reserve champion halter mare. The success of Circle J was a source of great pride for the whole Jaworski clan, who gathered at the ranch on most weekends, and managing the horse operation with Royce became another full-time job for me.

By 1970 a growing portion of the law firm's work was taking my colleagues and me out of Houston for extended periods. We had cases that took us regularly to the east and west coasts, and abroad. In addition, the board meetings of the insurance company were regularly held in exotic, fun places—an extension of the great times we had had in the fraternity at the University of Texas.

I worked with a cadre of bright, young trial lawyers who were emerging to be some of the best around—real highfliers. We had an absolute blast trying lawsuits, working hard, and "partying" hard to celebrate our successes. In addition, many of us had girlfriends in all of the places we visited. It was all part of the lifestyle, and I gave it very little thought. In those days, it was a kind of badge of honor to be successful in this particular realm, a mark of brotherhood, and was very well accepted among most of our contemporaries.

I'll never forget the celebration of a highly successful deposition—an episode which, although unique in one respect, was still fairly typical of the double life we were living.

At the conclusion of a deposition that successfully disposed of a major will contest in San Francisco, one of my young associates, Ken Wynne, and I stayed in town an extra night to celebrate. I invited Ken to come to Las Vegas the next day to attend one of the board meetings of our insurance company and have some fun with us.

He and I flew down to Las Vegas, and on Saturday morning we had our board meeting and worked until five o'clock. When the group gathered late that afternoon I said, "Look, why don't we all meet at the craps table at seven o'clock tonight? Ya'll bring your money with you because I feel it in my bones —I'm gonna really break the bank for you guys." There were thirteen of us around the craps table that evening. Now, I was not a great craps shooter, but I did enjoy it from time to time. I liked the thrill and the risk, and I had done some reading and knew a little bit about it.

So we were gathered around the table, and when the dice were passed to me, I said, "OK, you guys, get your money out there because you're in for a long ride." Honestly, I don't know why I was saying all this, but I felt it, and so I said it. After everybody got their money on the table, I threw the dice, and I crapped out. Everybody lost their money. The dice went to the next person, and everybody was hootin' and hollerin' at me and bitchin' and moanin'. So when the dice came around to me the next time, I said, "Okay, ye of little faith, everybody that's a true believer get your money back out there again because this is gonna be unbelievable. Get it out there and let's go."

Poor Kenny Wynne—he was a brand new lawyer with very little money, had something like twenty-five dollars with him, and had lost half of it on that first hand. So I said, "Kenny, put out the rest of your money." I rolled the dice, and I kept that one hand for forty-eight minutes. During that time, I was hitting everything on the board. The House had to stop the game twice to bring in more black chips. Toward the end, we had emptied the entire casino, and people were standing around our table fifteen and twenty deep. By that time I had my coat off and my sleeves rolled up, making pass after pass after pass. The noise was deafening, and it was just an electric situation. I was putting three or four hundred dollars on thirty-to-one odds for the croupiers, just as a tip to them. And I would roll snake-eyes or boxcars, and the proceeds from the roll went to them. I don't know how many times we did that.

By the time I rolled my last hand, the whole table was covered in black chips, stacked up high all over the numbers. When I made that final roll and crapped out, I don't know how many thousands upon thousands of dollars were on that table. But there was a huge war whoop when I made that last roll, and even though, of course, it was all over with, it had been an unbelievable experience. We all retired to the cocktail lounge where I bought drinks for the whole house. Later that next day, we took off for Houston and spent the day on the airplane counting our money.

>-+-◆-+-◯-+-◆-+-◄

Looking back at these years, it's difficult for me to understand how I could have maintained such a fragmented existence for so long without caving in to its incoherence and lack of central commitment. Life was an absolute blur—I was popping from one activity to another without a moment's hesitation to reflect and consider my overall life direction.

At the time, I considered this to be a great life, but in fact, I really didn't know life at all. Mine was a Disney World sort of life—inauthentic, narrow, utterly predictable, and largely devoid of any real meaning.

The end to this illusion would come to me, as it has for so many, by means of a personal crisis.

3. THE JOURNEY BEGINS

In 1975, when I was forty-one, my world came crashing down around me. I had been hunting at the ranch over Thanksgiving weekend with the Colonel and some business associates. On Sunday evening, I drove back to Houston and was just walking into my study to put down my gear when Fran came in and said, "Sit down, I've got something really important to tell you."

I sat down, and she said, "Joe, I want a divorce. There's somebody else that I love."

It was a complete surprise to me. She had been taking a class at the University of Houston, had met someone in the class, and had been seeing him.

After we talked, she said, "I want you to leave the house tonight." I don't remember much about that conversation; I guess I was in a state of total shock. But through the numbness, I felt a mixture of anger, confusion, betrayal, and fear. These came over me in great waves, but the overriding feeling was a complete and utter sense of disbelief and despair. My marriage of twenty years was over—bang, period, paragraph.

I packed up some bags and drove to a Howard Johnson's Motel on Interstate 10. The more remote it was, the better for me—I felt humiliated and didn't want anyone to see me. I was completely devastated and alone. Not only was I losing my wife and son, but the picture of my whole life had been shattered. It was if someone had taken a hammer and smashed it, destroying it in an instant.

>‑‹♦›‑O‑‹♦›‑‹

During those days of the separation and later, after the divorce, I went to my office and did my work, but early in the morning and late at night I remained alone, looking into myself and, in many ways, not liking what I saw. As I began to get in touch with myself and my feelings, the pain of my loss and confusion would well up in me and roll out. It would happen when I was reading, or writing, or sometimes when I was driving a car and thinking deeply, or walking somewhere. I kept hitting bottom—again and again—and the emotions would just flow out.

My older sister Joanie sensed the kind of pain I was in. One day after work I found a small package at my home. It was a book entitled *Notes to Myself*, by Hugh Prather, and inside was a note from Joanie saying that perhaps this book would help. I began reading it that evening and didn't put it down until I had finished it. Over the following days, I reread passage after passage from that little book. These were reflections by a person who had started on the path of self-discovery. He was trying to come to grips with who he was, why he was on a journey, and what that journey was all about. I could see from passage to passage how writing these notes helped the author to clarify things for himself, and how he developed a sort of therapy for himself from those insights.

I started writing in a similar fashion on sheets of loose paper, putting them into a file each day. Later I would look back and reread passages I had written months earlier. Over time I was amazed to see how I had changed, and how certain patterns had played out in my life. Sometimes I wouldn't look back at all. Just the process of reflecting, or spontaneously putting on paper feelings that were overwhelming me, helped. This process brought order to my mind and a kind of coherence to my consciousness. It also brought a peacefulness and understanding that I found in no other activity.

I then bought a journal of blank pages so that I could always keep these reflections for myself. Over time these dialogues with myself became very precious to me. Times of solitude became a kind of purification I needed in the midst of the crisis. As I look back, I realize that in those moments of silent dialogue—in the void—I gained important insights that helped guide me as I made choices about my life.

As my thoughts became clearer, I found myself spontaneously letting out my pain through deep, gut-wrenching crying. Maybe I was crying about the loss of my family—but I was also crying about the unreflective life I had led. And maybe I was releasing all the pent-up pain I had had over a number of years. But maybe it was just that for the first time, I was really allowing myself to feel. Until the divorce, I hadn't wept as an adult except briefly when my sister's son Mike had been killed in an automobile accident. Mike was very close to the Colonel, who saw him as his second chance to raise a son the right way. The Colonel spent a lot of time with Mike, listened to him, put his arms around him, and told him how much he loved and cared for him. And when Mike was killed, I believe it almost destroyed my father. He went into a tailspin, and he didn't really emerge for a couple of years. Almost immediately after the accident, I had to step into the breach and take care of all the arrangements because the Colonel was devastated. So I didn't have a whole lot of time to express my emotions. A few tears ran down my cheeks at that time, but that was just simple weeping. It hadn't been coming from the gut.

In the days and months that followed my separation and divorce, and over time, as I gradually began to open up to feeling, I also began to experience each day as precious. Previously I hadn't really experienced life that way. The years were a blur, with few real highs or lows. There were some great times, but strangely, I began to feel that it had been a pretty mediocre life. Now the peak experiences became so intense, they were burned into my memory, even though they weren't necessarily huge events. They could be very simple things, like early one Sunday morning in Paris just after the sun came up, when I came upon a small child feeding a pigeon in a little green square. Moments like these were sudden epiphanies of harmony that transfixed me. At first they were few and far between, but as time passed, they became more frequent and more accessible.

I began to reflect upon how I was living, where I was heading, and what I wanted out of life. In addition to writing in a journal, I was reading, and for the first time, I was thinking deeply about philosophical and personal issues. I talked to people as I traveled, people in my own generation and people who were older, trying to find out if the feelings I had about myself were shared by others. In fact, I found that most of the people in my generation who had achieved a great measure of success were feeling just as I was feeling: they had just about everything they wanted in terms of material goods, but they were not really living. They were not truly free. They wanted to step out and make a difference, they wanted to contribute, but they were immobilized by fear and by the need to have more and more material goods. It was the need to "have" instead of to "be." I discovered that people are not really afraid of dying; they're afraid of not ever having lived, not ever having deeply considered their life's higher purpose, and not ever having stepped into that purpose and at least tried to make a difference in this world.

It was to be years later as I looked back at this time of my life that I realized that this was the beginning of a new life journey for me, a journey that began within me. I didn't know it yet, but this was the opening moment of my taking a completely different path than I had previously taken, a new way of being. The essential elements of life were so different from before. Instead of controlling life, I ultimately learned what it meant to allow life to flow through me. Without the control, there are more intense highs and lows, and I felt much more at risk than ever before. But this sort of vulnerability goes with the path I'm describing—the path that reveals itself as we walk. But I'm getting ahead of myself, because in fact at this moment, little of this was very clear to me. These understandings were themselves being revealed to me very slowly over time. It was like a box within a box within a box.

4. FREEDOM

The days and months leading to the divorce were filled with trauma and emotions. These were extremely tough times for both Fran and me. We sought marriage counseling to help sort out our feelings and to determine if there was any chance of saving the marriage. We ultimately concluded there was none and moved forward with the divorce proceedings.

To our credit, we handled the necessary mechanics of the divorce in a relatively calm and mature way. One evening just before Christmas and only a month after I had moved out, we sat down in front of the fireplace and scratched out on three sheets of paper an outline reflecting how we would handle the property settlement, support, and custody issues. It was a reflective and loving moment in the midst of turbulent times for us both. We never deviated from that agreement.

In all this turmoil, I decided to sell the horse operation. I no longer wanted to devote every available weekend to Circle J—my heart just wasn't in it. The Colonel understood, so we agreed to hold a complete dispersal sale by auction on the afternoon of Sunday, February 15. The sale was held at the Civic Center Arena in the little town of San Marcos, Texas, which lay just south of Austin and only thirteen miles from the ranch.

The auction went beautifully. The crowd was large and enthusiastic, the horses were in terrific shape, and the auctioneer and sales management team did a fine job, all resulting in high averages for the entire sale. The hammer went down on the first horse at two-thirty that afternoon, and just five hours later, it was all over.

The decision to sell the horses was an emotional one for us all—it wasn't just the lives of our entire family that would be dramatically changed, but those of all the people who had made Circle J such a success over the past nine years. Most of these guys had been raised on West Texas ranches poking cattle for a living. They had eventually gravitated to working with horses, their first love, and their hard work had been the key to our success.

The seven of us were standing at the back of the sale barn. Everyone else had gone, and it was time to say goodbye. We stood around telling old "war" stories and had lots of laughs, but toward the end, we all grew misty-eyed. We had been through a lot together. It had been, as we said, "a great run."

Of all those gathered there that evening, Harold was taking it the hardest. Harold was one tough hombre. He was only about 160 pounds in his boots, but he was fast as lightning and hard as a rock. More than once I had gotten a call from Royce late at night for help to bail Harold out of a scrape for settling his differences with his fists. Harold had been only seventeen years old when he rode Magnolia Pay at the Fort Worth Rodeo and Livestock Show the night Pay won his final points for supreme champion.

Now it was all over. I made the rounds for the last time, shaking hands with each of the men. As I came to Harold, he just broke down, crying from the gut. I grabbed him and held him tight to me. Neither of us could talk for the longest time, but finally, through his tears, Harold said, "Why can't it be like it used to be? Why can't Fran be here with us? Why does it have to end this way?" As I held him, I just kept whispering in his ear, "I don't know, Harold, I just don't know."

The divorce was granted the following month. We continued for over two years thereafter to try to put things back together, but it was ultimately not to be. We found we had grown too far apart to ever make it work on a permanent basis.

By April 1976 I was living alone in the big house I had previously shared with Fran and Joey. Fran had moved to a smaller townhouse, and I was in the process of selling our home. At the law firm, I was in the midst of a major litigation, which was one of those all-consuming affairs. By early September, we had been in trial for thirteen weeks when the Court ordered a recess for seven weeks. I had cleared my docket and transferred all my other cases to other lawyers in the litigation section because this one case and the attendant litigations would occupy me for the next year or two. So when the recess came, I didn't have any immediate obligations, and for the first time in my adult life, I did something totally spontaneous. I packed a bag, bought a ticket to Paris, and took off to travel in Europe for those seven weeks. I had no game plan, made no prior arrangements, and packed very little. In my usual way of operating, this was highly unnatural; I was typically very methodical, planning every step of the way. I took a few books to reread—books I had discovered during the previous year that had made a deep impression on me. As it turned out, those books were instrumental in developing my thinking at that time.

As I was traveling in France, I found myself drawn to the cathedrals there, most particularly the great cathedral at Chartres, the small medieval town lying just southwest of Paris. This cathedral was built in the mid-thirteenth century when high gothic architecture was at its purest, and it possesses a unique symmetry and unity. Being near it and in it, I felt unity with all that was around me, a complete openness to the entire world. I intended to visit the cathedral for an hour or so, but ended up spending the entire day there, first sitting quietly and then later reflectively walking all around the vast cathedral, both inside and out.

As I was there, I experienced the most unusual feeling, a sort of ringing in my ears and entire head. It's difficult for me to describe, but it was distinctly familiar. It was as if I were in a different energy field altogether. I had experienced that feeling many times out in the wilderness, but this was the first time it had happened to me in a structure built by human hands.

Late that afternoon, still in the cathedral, I found myself thinking about two notions of freedom, both of which would be continually at play on this seven-week trip. The first was "freedom from," that is, freedom to get away from the oppressiveness of circumstances. A great deal of what I was experiencing was the need to break loose from the conformity of my life over the previous fifteen years as I fought the battle of living in the shadow of the Colonel. But another notion of freedom was beginning to make its way into my consciousness at this time, far below the surface—the freedom to follow my life's purpose with all the commitment I could muster, while at the same time, allowing life's creative forces to move through me without my control, without "making it happen." As I was to learn over time, this is by far a much more powerful way of operating.

The experience at Chartres made me want to find ways to break through the limiting factors I had discovered in myself, especially fear. One of the books I had taken with me to reread that helped me the most was *Jonathan Livingston Seagull*, by Richard Bach. To this day when I say the words "Jonathan Livingston Seagull," I can be carried back to the feelings I had when I first devoured that little book. I was driving down Interstate 10 from Houston to Austin on my way to a business meeting, and something so strong was compelling me to read it that I pulled over to a roadside park and began. As I read, I underlined passages, thinking, "Oh yes, oh yes, this is true."

One of the truths that Jonathan shared was "Break the chains of your thought, and you break the chains of your body, too." When I read those words, I felt they could be true for me, too. It sounded like such a pleasant fiction—but I knew it was the truth.

Jonathan knew so much about freedom because he knew about breaking the chains of conformity. The book is about the force that drove him to learn. It is about touching the highest part of ourselves and being driven to touch it again. It is about lifting ourselves out of ignorance and finding ourselves as creatures of excellence and intelligence and creativity. It is about discovering our higher purpose in life. I wanted so badly to discover that for myself. Why was I really here? What was it that I was really put on this earth to do? It is about overcoming boredom and fear and anger. It is about a capacity for new ways of knowing, or what Jonathan called "easy telepathy." It is about the principle that there is more to life than eating or fighting or power. It is about visualization, the process of imagining ourselves as a part of our ultimate dream—feeling it, touching it in our minds. It is about overcoming the fear of learning and the fear of seeing the godlike in ourselves.

I knew I had to have the freedom to be myself, my highest self, and that nothing could stand in my way if I really wanted it. This freedom is there for anyone who wants to discover it. The way is to change our level of consciousness, to change the way that we think about ourselves. If we have a taste of it, if we experience it, then we want to keep trying to practice, and eventually we find that unlimited being within.

5. GRAND PRIX TEST RUN

While spending a few days in Paris just wandering through parks, museums, cathedrals, and other quiet places, I continued thinking about the lessons I had learned from *Jonathan Livingston Seagull*. Occasionally, I would thumb through the book and read selected passages. I felt a strange sense of awe and joy in considering the questions, "What is my higher purpose in life? Why am I really here?" I had never considered these for myself. But, looking back, I realize I was unable to ponder very deeply such crucial life issues. In Paris I was only taking my first "baby steps" in this direction.

I also began to consider the question of how we might ever be able to fulfill an ultimate dream of ours. What would that process look like? How is it that we actually create new circumstances or a future that we envision? In taking another baby step, I began thinking—what if I set up a short-term challenge for myself that seemed impossible, but that I would go for and see if I could accomplish it? That would be a great experiment and a wonderful way to start off my European adventure! Ever since I was a teenager I had been fascinated by Ferraris, and in later years I enjoyed Grand Prix racing. By the mid-1970s, Ferrari had been involved in racing for around twenty-five years and had been enormously successful. Niki Lauda was driving that year for Ferrari. Above anything else, I wanted to go to the Grand Prix at Monza, Italy, and be there in the pits with Lauda and the Ferrari racing team. That would be my challenge.

I began calling the factory in Modena and telexing various acquaintances in the United States to see if anyone could help get me any tickets to the Italian Grand Prix. Finally, a close friend of mine opened the door for me to contact Dr. Gotti, who was a senior executive at Ferrari. Gotti told me that it was absolutely impossible to get any tickets to the Grand Prix. All the seats had been completely sold-out for over six months, and for the last several months, only infield tickets were available. He said there would be over two hundred thousand people in the infield alone. He said it was dangerous, and the crowd surge might engulf people; riots could break out on the infield. He said the race actually started on September 12, but that people camped out at least two days in advance to get in. Just to get out there, to fight through the crowds, one would have to leave Milan by train at eight in the morning to be there in time for the three-thirty race that afternoon. He felt it would be impossible to get in. But I was determined to go to the race and to fulfill my dream of being in the pits next to Lauda prior to the beginning of the race.

I went to Milan and spent the night there, but when I woke up at four in the morning, rain was pouring down. I was dismayed because I knew there was a long walk from the train station in Monza to the Autodroma—at least forty-five minutes. I would be drenched to the bone if I had no raingear, and I knew it was crazy to stay soaked all day and into the evening. There were no shops open at that time in the morning, so I sat down in the lobby and began trying to figure out what my next step would be.

I looked up, and there was a man about my size who was just walking over to the reception desk. He had a raincoat and an umbrella. I went over to him and touched him on the elbow. As he turned around, I looked him straight in the eye and said, "Pardon me for bothering you, sir, but my name is Joe Jaworski; I'm from Houston, and I need your raincoat and umbrella for the day."

He didn't say anything, so I went on. "I'm going out to the race at Monza, and I left my raincoat and umbrella in Switzerland. It's really important that I get out there right away. Please let me borrow your umbrella and raincoat, and I promise you I'll bring them back tomorrow."

He looked at me a moment more, and then with a half-smile, he said, "Sure, why not?" He put his briefcase down, took off his raincoat, handed it to me, and said, "I'm Manny Deitz. I'll be here for a couple of days. Give me a call tomorrow when you get back." He gave me his card, and I told him how deeply grateful I was. Then I was off.

As I made my way out to the Autodroma Nazionale Di Monza, I couldn't believe my eyes. There were hordes of people streaming into the area. I wrote in my journal, "I can describe it only as ten times the Super Bowl. If Rice Stadium holds eighty-five thousand, there must have been half a million people out there." What a challenge. I cased the area for over an hour. I thought about every conceivable way to get inside. There were guard dogs, high fences with barbed wire, police and soldiers everywhere. I first went to the most imposing area I could find, the VIP entrance. They called it the "Tribune" entrance. It was guarded by a high-ranking military officer. I tried to talk my way in there and almost succeeded, but an officer they referred to as "Generalissimo" finally came and ultimately turned me away.

I next went over to the area where all of the television trucks were located, thinking I might impersonate a television sportscaster. This involved a kind of deception I would find unacceptable now. But at that stage of my development I simply operated at a different level. (Part of my developmental path has been to learn compassion, including compassion toward myself for my earlier shortcomings.)

I began gathering information by talking to workers around the television trucks, and then talking to some of their superiors. I finally went up to the entrance to the press room and told the guard that I needed to see the secretary of the press corps. I was shown up to the office and told the people there that I was a CBS correspondent. I had left my pass at the hotel and I had come all the way from Texas and needed only to gain access to the pits in order to find my colleagues. I spent thirty minutes chatting with them. The secretary of the press corps at one point said she had only one pass left that she was holding for a correspondent from Spain whom she was expecting momentarily. She took it out of her purse and held it. I looked into her eyes and said, "I really need this." She stood there momentarily and then reached behind her and pulled an extra pass from a file and handed it to me. I kissed her on the cheek and was off.

It was a huge green plastic pass that was hung around your neck. You could go anywhere with it. I ran down to the main entrance and walked in past the guard dogs, the officials, the police, and the army. I first went to the "ready area" where all of the formula one cars were being prepared and fueled. I stood next to Niki Lauda's Ferrari, then Jody Schekter's Tyrrell, and Clay Regazzoni's Ferrari 312-T. There was a businesslike atmosphere in the ready area, but with more to it than just a quiet efficiency. I couldn't quite put my finger on what I felt there, but I was absolutely drawn to the drama that was about to unfold.

It was close to race time, so I went down to the private sponsors' dining rooms near the ready area for some lunch. I met a number of people but hurried though lunch in order to go back to the pits before the race. As I was leaving, a man walked up and introduced himself. He was French but spoke excellent English. His name was Bernard Cahier, President of the International Racing Press Association, headquartered in Paris. He told me that rather than taking a seat in the sponsors' area, which was a comfortable but detached way to watch the race, I should find the best vantage points to see the race—and he showed me what these were. Cahier particularly recommended a certain spot at the Curva Parabolica. I thanked him warmly for his help and then quickly went back over to the pits to be with the drivers and their teams.

Just before the beginning of the race, I watched as the different teams pushed the cars from the pits onto the track, where the cars were "gridded out" in a series of staggered rows with the fastest driver in practice occupying the "pole" position. The few minutes just before the flag dropped were very special—in these moments seemed to be crystalized all the drama, tension, and expectancy that make up the attraction of motor racing. There was a great deal of activity at this moment on the grid, but in a way, in the midst of all the noise in the grandstands, a kind of quiet pervaded the area of the grid. I was about ten feet from Lauda when he entered his car. I noticed his eyes as he was looking out of his helmet, and I felt I saw real fear there, but also fierce determination. Here was a man who, six weeks before, had almost been destroyed in a terrible crash and was now making his return to the track. There seemed to be a special energy out there on the grid—and for a moment I thought it strangely seemed like my experience at Chartres.

After the start, I made my way over to the place at the Curva Parabolica that Cahier had suggested. It was a fine vantage point, and from there I watched as the race began to settle into its own rhythm. The leaders widened a gap between themselves and the rest of the field, and an order began to take shape as the race took on a collective flow. From my vantage point I could watch the lines the various drivers took through this corner using literally every inch of the track. I could also clearly see the dicing that took place at the corner as drivers sought to pass one another at high speed when their cars were only inches apart. Being there was a deeply enjoyable experience for me.

>⊷⊶•○•⊷⊶<

The next day I found Manny Deitz so I could return his raincoat and umbrella. I told him how much I appreciated what he had done and invited him for lunch. At lunch that day, he told me his story.

In World War II, Manny was a fighter pilot for the American Air Force. During a dogfight off the coast of Italy, he shot down an Italian plane whose pilot managed to parachute out. Instead of flying off, which he probably should have done since he had a limited amount of fuel, Manny waited to make sure the pilot's life vest was fully inflated and that he was okay. Then he radioed for help for the downed pilot, and he circled around until it got there. When our people finally reached the flyer, Manny made a low pass and gave him the thumbs-up sign, and the Italian returned it. As he flew off, Manny wagged his wings as if to say goodbye.

When the war ended, Manny went back to Philadelphia. One day, a letter came from the Italian flyer, who had tracked Manny down from the number on the plane's wings. The flyer asked if he could come see him, and Manny said yes. When they finally met, the Italian said, "You know, you saved my life, and I feel as if I would like to stay connected to you. I'd like for us to work together. My family has a leather goods factory that makes shoes and purses. Would you be my partner? We could start a branch over in the States." So ever since the war, this Italian and Manny have been co-owners of a successful manufacturing business in shoes and handbags made in Italy and marketed in Europe and the United States, and they've been the best of friends as well as business partners.

I've thought a great deal about Manny and his story and about the race I had seen and about all that had happened. I now know that this adventure was an important early step toward significant learning later in my life.

In the first place, years later in life it provided a kind of landmark in memory of how *not* to operate as we move to create new circumstances. Yes, it's important to see the world as full of possibilities—to shift our world view from one of resignation to one of possibility. But if we are to participate in the unfolding process of the universe, we must let life *flow* through us, rather than attempt to *control* life. Again, my usual pattern had been just the contrary: to commit to something and then move to fulfill that commitment at all costs, to do whatever it took to "make it happen." That's exactly what had happened at the Grand Prix—I had even resorted to deception when the possibility of success looked least likely. As I was to learn over the ensuing years, this is a much less powerful way of operating in life.

This experience also provided some early insight into what I later understood as the collective state of flow. Back then, it wasn't entirely clear what had attracted me so strongly to that motor race, but I knew something about the state of consciousness people achieve when they are so engaged in an activity that nothing else seems to matter. The experience in and of itself is so rare and so enjoyable that people will seek to replicate it at great cost—even at the risk of life itself—just for the sake of having it again. I later came to know this as the "flow state." I had experienced this state of flow myself from time to time while listening to music, writing in my journal, running, and backpacking in the wilderness. What attracted me to motor racing was the desire to be near people who were experiencing the flow state *together* in dramatic and unmistakable circumstances, and where one interruption in the flow could mean death.

To see drivers pass one another around corners approaching two hundred miles per hour at extremely close tolerances is an astonishing and singular experience. It's true that a high degree of skill, sensitive control, and good judgment are a prerequisite at this level of the sport, but there is far more to it than that. In professional racing there is a code between drivers that allows close passing with a minimum of danger. It's not often discussed, but all professional drivers at some level recognize the altered state of consciousness that occurs during a high speed race. Relatively few drivers have the language to describe these flow states, and very little of it finds its way into their biographies or their reports to the news media.

In this state there is an extraordinary clarity, focus, and concentration. The flow of time is altered. The world champion Jackie Stewart once described it as an uncanny sense of everything in the race slowing down, as if everyone was moving in slow motion, thus permitting him to make maneuvers that would be impossible in his ordinary state.

And finally, this adventure provided to me the gift of Manny Deitz. It was a gift of many aspects. His appearance in the lobby at four-thirty in the morning when I needed him; his absolute trust in me; and, of course, his story, which spoke so clearly to me about how love and human connectedness can transcend even the circumstance of two fighter pilots locked in mortal combat. At one level it seemed such an unlikely story—yet at another level it seemed not surprising at all to me. This was another guiding event, preparing me for the shift of mind that would eventually allow me to see relationship as the organizing principle of the universe.

6. THE ART OF LOVING

I spent a lot of time on this journey in Europe by myself, just reading, thinking, and writing in my journal. One of the books I read and reread, trying to figure out why I had been so oblivious to what was going on in my marriage, was Eric Fromm's *The Art of Loving*. Fromm's thesis is that love is the only satisfactory answer to the problem of human existence. Loving is an art, and we must master not only the theory of love but also the practice of love.

I learned that our deepest need is to overcome our aloneness and our separateness. We seek to escape from separateness in various ways. We seek conformity, mistaking it for union. This is a soul-crushing way to exist. Or we seek union through orgiastic states—drugs, alcoholism, overwork—or through creative activities. But the ultimate escape from separateness is through interpersonal union.

Fromm writes that mature love is union under the condition of preserving one's integrity and individuality. The paradox: two beings become one and yet remain two. Giving is the highest expression of potency. Fromm sets forth the elements of love: care, which is active concern for the life and growth of the one we love; responsibility, which is caring for one's physical needs as well as one's higher needs; and respect, which is allowing others to grow as they need to on their own terms.

He speaks of the types of love—erotic love, parental love, self-love, love of God, and brotherly love. And I learned of Fromm's admonition: To learn to love is not easy. It requires discipline in one's whole life. It requires concentration, aloneness, thought, knowledge of oneself, listening, living in the present, patience. Above all, to love must be your supreme concern.

Although I enjoyed being alone and reading on this trip, I sometimes wanted to be with people, and when I did, without really trying, I would encounter remarkable people. Much later I realized there was an openness and a vulnerability within me that allowed me to connect with people in a way and at a level that I had never experienced before. It was all part of my experiment with trust of and *patience* with the natural flow of life, with being open to the next step, and then taking it when the moment seemed right.

On the last week of my trip, I arrived in Cannes and went to dinner at Felix, a small restaurant recommended to me. I felt open, full of life, and peaceful. I had great exchanges with the proprietor and the person behind the bar. I was rereading *The Art of Loving*, studying all I had read, trying to comprehend and integrate it. From time to time I would put the book down and study people as they walked down the sidewalk. One of them was an attractive young woman with big brown eyes who walked very briskly down the sidewalk and past my table. As she walked by, we smiled at one another. About ten minutes later, as I was reading my book, I looked up, and she was standing beside my table. She had come back to the restaurant and asked if she could sit down and have dinner with me, paying her own part. I could tell she was frightened a little bit by what she was doing, and I stood up and asked her to sit down. We had dinner, we talked, we drank wine, and we walked by the shore.

Her name was Bernadette. She was a very natural person who wore no makeup at all. She was a businesswoman from New York who was on a month-long holiday prior to an important meeting in Paris. She was well read, articulate, and gentle. She was a genuinely beautiful person in a deep way.

We spent a marvelous several days together. A lot of it was fun and sightseeing. But the play became secondary; a lot of the time we shared was very serious, philosophizing and talking together. We talked about what was important in life. We talked about what drew us together. She said it was our eyes meeting and the aura that I was radiating. She had never before in her life gone over to a strange man and invited herself for dinner. But she felt drawn to do so, almost compelled to do so. She was lonely and frightened, thinking about the importance of the meeting she was to have in Paris in a few days. I had toyed with the idea of going to Paris with her, but that was put to rest when I received a telex from my office informing me that the trial was to resume, and I had to return.

The day Bernadette was to fly to Paris, she came to my hotel room. It was a Sunday morning, and I was sitting on the veranda, soaking up the sun and watching a regatta out in the bay. There must have been a hundred sail boats preparing for the competition. I was listening to beautiful music and was very content and happy, alone with my thoughts and memories, restful and peaceful. Bernadette came to my door. She said she had to see me one more time to tell me what the last few days had meant to her. She said I had deeply touched her life, very much like Jonathan had Fletcher Seagull. She found she was no longer anxious about the meeting in Paris. She was prepared to take a new direction in her life, even if it might adversely affect her career. In ten minutes she was gone. I felt I might never see her again.

As I sat in my room, tears were running down my cheeks. It was not out of sadness that I wept, but because of the realization that I had had a profound effect on someone else's life. That was the first experience of its kind for me. And I knew why I had been able to help her—it was because her well-being was a matter of my ultimate concern. I had given to Bernadette my interest, my understanding, my knowledge, and all that was alive in me. I had given my life to her for a few days and apparently had enriched her life, while at the same time enhancing my own. I was also touched very deeply by the way we had met, and her display of courage in coming to me in the first place that night—the trembling in her voice as she spoke to me, her openness, her honesty.

><+>-○-<+><

I was also deeply affected by the way my relationship with Bernadette had developed and what it stood for. This whole encounter was an expression of a new kind of freedom for me. At this stage of my life, my first instinct would have been to position myself to relate to her in a sexual way—to angle for a way to connect with her physically. But from almost the first moment she sat down with me, the physical attraction was secondary. There was a deeper part of me that knew this meeting was not about romance. We were connecting on an entirely different level, as two people touching one another and transcending boundaries in a more profound and lasting way. It was as if I had been given a gift that allowed me to put Fromm's principles into practice for this brief moment of my life.

Although I was to see Bernadette only one other time in my life, the lesson that I learned from this encounter was life changing. The alchemy of Fromm's teachings and my experience with Bernadette provided for me a key insight: when we are in this state of being where we are open to life and all its possibilities, willing to take the next step as it is presented to us, then we meet the most remarkable people who are important contributors to our life. This occurs in part through the meeting of our eyes; it's as if our souls instantly connect, so that we become part of a life together at that moment. This is not at all about sexuality, nor about maleness and femaleness. It's about human beings connecting. At once there is an instant trust and intimacy—we belong with the other for a moment. It is a spiritual connection that is not limited to our meeting one person. Once such an encounter happens to you in this open state, it will happen again. And when it happens, you know it immediately, for it's a very special phenomenon. It's as if you and the other are in the same family. Although I didn't understand it at the time, this is precisely what occurred between Manny Deitz and me in Milan, when he gave me, a perfect "stranger," his expensive raincoat.

I have a close friend, a highly regarded educator—let's call her Mary—who operates in this state of being for all aspects of her life. Mary told me of an occasion when she was riding the London subway and a family of four, which included a girl who appeared to be about ten years old, sat down across from her. As the young girl sat down, Mary's eyes met the girl's for an instant. Within moments, the girl got up, crossed the subway car, and sat in an empty seat next to Mary. Mary knew what had occurred. Nothing was said as they sat next to one another, but Mary told me how much she appreciated that this young girl had acted on the impulse she had when their eyes had met, that she made this gesture toward Mary, acknowledging what was unspoken.

All too often this meeting of the eyes occurs, and we don't act on it. Another friend of mine was traveling in Argentina more than fifteen years ago. While he was in Buenos Aires, his eyes met a woman's as they passed on the street. Instantly he felt he knew her, but he didn't turn back to meet her. He's been haunted by this failure to act ever since, wondering what might have been.

The more open we are, the more these encounters occur. The physical meetings that result from these encounters can last for ten minutes (Mary's did on the subway), for a day (as mine did with Manny), for several days (as mine did with Bernadette), or for a lifetime (as you will see from a story I'll tell later). But in another sense all of the meetings are forever because they are deep and meaningful encounters that we always hold close.

>-·-◇-○-◇-·-<

Alone in Europe, I had begun to reflect on the larger purpose of my life, and what I wanted out of it. I realized that I wanted to broaden my perspective and perhaps find a way to contribute to the larger social enterprise, not just in my narrow little niche in the practice of law. The more I thought about it, the more I realized how much I wanted to do this. And yet I found that I was afraid. I was afraid to step out of my own little tribe, my own little narrow circle. I was afraid to take the risk of stepping into anything unknown. And most importantly, I was afraid that I just couldn't make any difference anyway. I could barely get my arms around the issues related to building the law firm and trying lawsuits. How could I possibly get my arms around the issues facing our community or our nation? I felt powerless, and so I just hung back. I didn't feel qualified, and I didn't have the linkages outside of my own little group. I didn't have any support group to speak of, I was out of touch with anyone but lawyers, and I basically felt isolated.

7. ONENESS

How are we educated by children, by animals! . . .
We live in the currents of universal reciprocity.

—Martin Buber

After the trial concluded, I went backpacking up in the Grand Teton
Mountains. I had planned the trip for early September, but the trial had interfered,
and instead of canceling, I decided to go in late October. I had been told that the
snow would be heavy and it could be a difficult trip, but that was the only time I
had. So I found a guide, Paul Lawrence, who had done photography work for
magazines and knew about the Tetons during the winter.

Paul and I were at eleven thousand feet near Hurricane Pass between Cascade
Canyon and Alaska Basin in the Tetons. It was almost noon on Friday, October 21.
I was taking in the spectacular scenery—the Grand Teton itself, the snow-covered
passes, crystal clear streams and brooks, running falls, icicle falls, snowshoe rabbits,
and bright blue skies. At this time of year, no one else was backpacking in the
mountains. We were totally alone.

The third day out, I got up early in the morning to fish in a stream not far from
our camp. As I walked along, suddenly in front of me a beautiful ermine popped out
of the deep snow. She couldn't have been more than ten feet from me. All at once
she appeared with her almost black eyes looking directly into mine. I stopped in my
tracks. She sat there staring straight at me, moving not a whisker or a muscle. It
seems as if we looked into one another's eyes for several minutes, but perhaps it was
less than one. She turned to go but stopped, turned around again, and took another
long look at me. Then she began. She jumped up into the air and did a huge flip,

and then looked into my eyes again, as if to say, "What did you think about that?" She did this same trick for me three or four times, each time cocking her head to the side and looking at me as if to ask for my approval. I stood there, held transfixed. Then I began smiling and cocking my head in the same direction as hers. This went on for the longest time. There together, I felt at one with that ermine. Finally, when she had finished, she turned around once more and looked at me, then went down into the snow again and was gone.

I stayed in that spot for the longest time, alone, considering the experience. I knew then that it was a profound experience and consider it so to this day. We communicated, that ermine and I, and for those few moments, I experienced what I can only describe as a kind of transcendence of time and a feeling of oneness with all the universe.

>−+◆>−○−◆+−<

I thought a great deal about my encounter with the ermine. But it was to be a long time before I was able to comprehend how important it truly was for me. It was much more significant than it might seem on the surface.

What it taught me was the importance of the experience of oneness. Throughout my childhood I cannot recall ever having felt this fundamental accord with another. Perhaps this capacity was squeezed out of me by socialization at an early date. Perhaps it's because oneness was not valued or encouraged in my own family—it simply was not within my parents' world view.

The first time that I can ever recall feeling this unity with another was in the midst of crisis. I was nineteen years old and a student at Baylor University in Waco, Texas. At four forty-five one afternoon, a killer tornado, packing winds of over five hundred miles per hour, ripped through the town. It sounded like a hundred freight trains roaring through the streets, and in what seemed an instant, when it was over, there was a deadly silence. I ventured out from my dormitory and within just a few short blocks, I began walking through the devastation. The baseball park had vanished. The post office looked as if it had been sliced down the middle by a huge cleaver. As I walked another block, I saw where a large furniture store had been. All of the stories had simply collapsed into the basement, and there was now just a large pile of rubble. It was a numbing experience to realize what had happened to the hundreds of people on those floors. One hundred and fourteen people died in those few minutes; hundreds more were severely injured. I went to work that afternoon and spent the next three days pulling people, alive and dead, out of the rubble. I began feeling at one with the other workers, and with the people I pulled out and carried to the makeshift hospital or to the morgue. There was no separation among us in the midst of all that suffering, just a sense of accord.

I experienced this sense again a few years later. Late one night I was riding around the ranch in our open-top Jeep. Mike McDonald, one of my close friends, was riding in the front seat with me. We were traveling in an open field with high grass, and it was so dark we didn't see a huge boulder in the middle of the field. We struck the boulder and the Jeep flipped. When I came to, I was pinned under the hood of the overturned Jeep, and Mike was leaning over me, his face close to mine. My chest was being crushed, and I could barely get the words out—"Mike, I'm dying, I can't breathe. You've got to get this off of me." Mike weighed about a hundred and thirty pounds dripping wet. In the beam of the headlights, I could see him gazing into my eyes. He didn't say anything. At that moment I felt we were two aspects of one life.

Without saying a word, Mike moved to the front of the Jeep where the bumper was, planted his feet firmly on the ground, and picked the Jeep up a few inches. I was able to slide free, and when I was out, Mike collapsed to the ground.

Sometimes the oneness happens between a lawyer and a jury. I've talked to many of the best trial lawyers, and they acknowledge that there is often a moment, either in the closing argument or the trial itself, where there is nothing between you and the jury. You're a part of them, and they're a part of you.

I recall trying one particularly difficult lawsuit with a young associate of mine who rose to be one of the top trial partners at our firm. At the summation, we were opposed by a trial lawyer from one of the largest firms in Houston, a man who is acknowledged to be one of the four or five best lawyers in the state. His opening, in which he raked my associate over the coals, was scathing. When his argument was completed, I realized that his strategy had been effective and his delivery flawless. But what he had said was wrong, and I felt he was not entitled to win this litigation. I stood up and looked at the jury and laid aside all of the prepared notes that we had worked on so hard. I began speaking straight from the heart and was operating on a level that was higher and totally different from the normal, rational, linear plane represented by the days of work that had gone into my prepared remarks. I hardly remember what I said, but when it was over, there were tears in my eyes and tears running down the cheeks of many of the jurors. We won that lawsuit against all odds. Most observers said it was because of the final argument. All I know was that at the moment I stood before the jury, I had a feeling of accord with my young associate, my client, and all of the members of the jury. As I look back on my experience as a litigator, I realize that my very best performances occurred when I operated at this level. My very worst performances happened when I operated at a purely rational level.

Several months after the trip to the Tetons, I ran into Fran Tarkenton, the former quarterback of the Minnesota Vikings, and we talked at length about connections between sports and the mind. Tarkenton told me story after story about his altered states of consciousness as he played football. He talked about how he would "see" the ball in the hands of the receiver before the play would ever run. He would look at his receiver and call the play, and the two of them would see the play as having been completed. As he would begin to run the play, he would have a kind of clarity that he said was hard to describe. He and the receiver were in complete accord. Things would slow down and be almost effortless. He knew before the ball ever left his hands that it was a completed pass.

What Tarkenton told me helped me to see what happened in my encounter with the ermine. I had so many deep feelings about that encounter, especially about how the world is fundamentally inseparable. It was so important to me, but it made me self-conscious to talk about it. Instead, I would often quote from Bill Russell's book *Second Wind*, which describes the feeling of oneness I had experienced, but in the more acceptable terms of sport:

> Every so often a Celtic game would heat up so that it became more than a physical or even a mental game, and would be magical. That feeling is very difficult to describe, and I certainly never talked about it when I was playing. When it happened, I could feel my play rise to a new level. It came rarely, and would last anywhere from five minutes to a whole quarter or more. . . . It would surround not only me and the other Celtics, but also the players on the other team, even the referees.

> At that special level, all sorts of odd things happened. The game would be in a white heat of competition, and yet somehow I wouldn't feel

competitive—which is a miracle in itself. I'd be putting out the maximum effort, straining, coughing up parts of my lungs as we ran, and yet I never felt the pain. The game would move so quickly that every fake, cut and pass would be surprising, and yet nothing could surprise me. It was almost as if we were playing in slow motion. During those spells, I could almost sense how the next play would develop and where the next shot would be taken. . . . My premonitions would be consistently correct, and I always felt then that I not only knew all of the Celtics by heart, but also all the opposing players, and that they all knew me. There have been many times in my career when I felt moved or joyful, but these were the moments when I had chills pulsing up and down my spine.

Much later, as I began to comprehend more about what happened that morning in the Tetons, I was more comfortable speaking directly to the issue. I realized that these experiences of oneness—in Waco after the tornado, with Mike after the Jeep accident, during the jury argument—were all significant; but the experience with Bernadette and later with the ermine were watershed events in my life. The occasion with Bernadette was the first time that an entirely new orientation was involved. It was what the philosopher Martin Buber spoke of as the *I and Thou* orientation—treating another as a "Thou" rather than as an "It." Boundaries were transcended in a way we don't ordinarily expect. This created a new opening for me in my life, an emerging awareness about the impermanence of boundaries and an opportunity to change my whole orientation about the possibilities of dialogue and interaction with others.

When I encountered the ermine, there was also a transcendence of boundaries that we don't ordinarily expect in our lifetime—a loss of boundaries with part of the natural world. It was as if for those few moments we were inseparably fused. I was drawn into a relation with the ermine, and she was not an "other" to me. I know now that my orientation had shifted, and that was what had made it possible to encounter the ermine herself.

This provided me with new clarity. I had had a direct contact with an aspect of the natural world which my lifelong, fragmented perspective had previously said was not open to me. This forced a shift in conscious functioning and began to prepare me at a deep level to recognize the impermanence and transparency of boundaries in all other aspects of my existence. This shift didn't happen overnight—it was like a time-release capsule, with the shift occurring over the ensuing years. Over time I came to see that the boundaries we create in this life are imaginary; they don't exist, but we create them. Then we feel trapped by them.

This type of awareness—sometimes called "unity consciousness"—is natural to human beings, but because of early socialization, we progressively limit our world. We turn from our true nature to embrace boundaries in all sorts of ways. The encounter with the ermine was so important to me because it was the first time I had directly experienced the interrelatedness of the universe.

8. THE DREAM

The Way to do is to be.

—Lao-Tzu

Over the next several months, I kept reflecting on my experiences in Europe and with the ermine up in the mountains. I couldn't talk with anyone about these experiences; I had a hard time even comprehending them myself. I continued to have similar experiences involving the loss of boundaries where my sense of identity expanded to include God and the entire universe. I had been taught to pray since early childhood, but this loss of boundary between God and me was too much to comprehend. I went to a close friend, who was one of Houston's best known psychiatrists, to see if he could assure me that I wasn't going off the deep end. I told him the whole story—all of what had been occurring over the past year or so. He chuckled and gave me the assurance I needed. He also gave me some books that described this type of experience, and I discovered how it is central to every major religion, including Judaism, Islam, Christianity, Hinduism, Buddhism, and Taoism. This helped me feel more comfortable with the phenomenon, but I still couldn't fully comprehend the mystery of it. I knew there was a new awareness growing within me, and I felt deep down there was much more to come.

Over time, I began to feel that the organizing principle of the universe is "relatedness," and that this is more fundamental than "thingness." It kept occurring to me that this new understanding is what's missing in how we think about leadership. We're always talking about what leaders *do*—about leadership style and function—but we put very little emphasis on the *being* aspect of leadership.

My experience in Europe reading Fromm's *The Art of Loving* led me to read Fromm's next book, *To Have or To Be*. Fromm's thesis could be summed up by the two quotes that appeared at the introduction to his book:

> The Way to do is to be.
> —Lao-Tzu

> People should not consider so much what they are to *do*, as what they *are*.
> —Meister Eckhart

Fromm explains that Being is a fundamental mode of existence or orientation to the world, one of aliveness and authentic relatedness. It has to do with our character, our total orientation to life; it is a state of inner activity. For the first time in history, he argues, the physical survival of the human race depends on a radical change of the human heart. This is a call to service that will take great courage—to leave what we *have* and move out, not without fear, but without succumbing to that fear. It is a call to redefine what is possible, to see a vision of a new world and to be willing to undertake, step-by-step, what is necessary in concrete terms to achieve that vision.

▸┄◂▸┄○┄◂▸┄◂

A few weeks later, as I was reading everything I could find on the subject of leadership, I received a pamphlet in the mail with a simple essay inside written by Robert Greenleaf. It was a thin little pamphlet, only thirty-seven pages long, with a burnt orange cover, entitled *The Servant as Leader*. I wish I could remember who sent it to me because I owe that person an eternal debt of gratitude. The moment I saw the words "Servant as Leader," they had an enormous impact on me. The very notion of servant leadership was absolutely stunning to me, and I couldn't put it out of my mind. It was as if someone had suddenly cleansed my lens of perception, enabling me to understand what I had been struggling with for so long; at the same time, it was as if a memory of long ago was being reawakened. With his words, Greenleaf took me by the hand and opened a pathway for me to territory I'm still experiencing to this day, some nineteen years later.

Greenleaf attributed the idea of servant leadership to Herman Hesse's book *Journey to the East*. The narrator of the story is on a journey with a band of men, looking for enlightenment (a journey probably intended to symbolize Hesse's own,

Greenleaf pointed out). Leo is the servant who does the group's menial chores, but who also sustains them with his presence, his spirit, and his song. The journey lasts for years, and all goes well through all kinds of travail until Leo disappears. The group finds they cannot make it without Leo. They fall into disarray, they become lost, and the narrator almost dies. After years of wandering, the narrator finally finds Leo and is taken to the order that sponsored the journey. There, Greenleaf says, he discovers that Leo, whom he had first known as *servant*, was actually the head of the order, its guiding spirit, a great and noble *leader*. Leo, by the quality of the inner life that was expressed by his presence, had served to lift the group up and make their journey possible.

In this essay, Greenleaf takes a fundamental stand and sets forth a new framework through which we can understand the underlying dynamics of leadership. The essence of leadership, says Greenleaf, is the desire to serve one another and to serve something beyond ourselves, a higher purpose. In our traditional way of thinking, "servant leadership" sounds like an oxymoron. But in a world of relationships, where relatedness is the organizing principle of the universe, it makes perfect sense. In that orientation, servant leadership seems like a very potent and natural way to think about leadership. This, I began to realize, was a critical piece to the puzzle I had been struggling with for so long.

><+<>+<0+<<>+><

Everything in me was saying I had to get away to digest all that had been happening to me and to understand what was trying to emerge. So, armed with these ideas, in early 1977 I took off for a couple of weeks and went to the mountains again, this time to Steamboat Springs, Colorado, to deliberately practice the art of solitude and to consider all that was before me.

It was late spring—to me the most beautiful time in the mountains, a time of birth and renewal. I stayed at a private condominium that lay high up the western edge of the ski area (which at this time of year was closed), within a few minutes' walk of some unimproved property I had purchased during the previous ski season.

Every morning I would get up just before daybreak, have juice and fruit, stretch, and take a long, slow run in the mountains. After returning for a shower and breakfast, I would make my way up to the property and spend the day there writing and thinking. Once there, I felt completely alone, as if on the top of the world. The property was surrounded by greenbelt and natural forest and had a kind of eagle's nest feel to it, being the highest point in the immediate area. Off to the east, the view was directly up the ski mountain, and below to the west, I could see the entire Yampa Valley and all that lay beyond for forty or fifty miles. It was a spectacular place to be that spring, there among the wildflowers and tall pines and firs.

By the time I left the mountains, I had a basic outline for an institute that would develop servant leadership. Eventually, I would call it the American Leadership Forum. It would be patterned in some ways after the well-known White House Fellows Program, but it would encourage linkages among different sectors of society and the rising generation of leaders in a community or region. It would heighten their sense of public responsibility, and it would enhance their capacity to lead in a pluralistic society where no one would ever be "in charge" again. The overarching principle of the organization would be one of servant leadership, serving with compassion and heart, and recognizing that the only true authority for this new era is that which enriches participants, and empowers rather than dimishes them. It would encourage "transformational leadership": leadership of strong commitment and broad visionary ideas. It would be creative leadership rather than reactive leadership. It would be leadership with the capacity to imagine a great community or a great region and the capacity to help make that greatness happen. It would embrace the notion that we don't have to be bound by our current circumstances, but that we can literally choose the kind of community, the kind of world, that we want to live in.

Bringing the Leadership Forum to reality would require a search for hidden talent. I felt there were hundreds of world-class leaders, men and women of the successor generation, younger people who were just a step away from the top. It would be our task to encourage them to see their larger purposes, to see their special destinies in life, and to reach for that which was truly worthy of them. We were on the threshold of a new era, and we had to shape it to the highest purposes and the highest values we could. Above all, we had to strive to understand the meaning of kindness and love, "the perfect and visible principle of all life." I remembered these words from *Jonathan Livingston Seagull*, and the last words of Jonathan's teacher, Chiang, as he disappeared in a flash of brilliant light: "Jonathan, keep working on love." That became my overall quest in life and the very bedrock on which the American Leadership Forum was to be founded—the idea of service to and compassion for others. The idea of servant leadership. The idea of helping others in their struggle to break free of their limits. It became my personal mission to share with others something of the truth that was unfolding before me.

I held the idea of the American Leadership Forum close to my vest for about six months. It was such a large dream that I was afraid to tell anyone because it seemed so grandiose. I almost felt ashamed that I could even imagine myself doing something like this.

A year later, a client and very close friend of mine, Tom Fatjo, came to see me. Tom, the founder of Browning & Ferris Industries (better known now as BFI), was an accountant who was also a great entrepreneur. He had come up with an idea about the way that solid waste and trash could be handled. After devising the system, he bought a garbage truck, and then got up at four o'clock every morning to ride on the back of the truck and pick up the trash in his neighborhood to test his system. Out of his idea has grown one of the largest solid waste management firms in the world.

Tom came to my office to share his dream with me about an executive development center which would be located in Houston and which would be dedicated to helping business executives and professionals achieve a more productive quality of life. As he shared his dream with me, it encouraged me to feel that I could tell him about mine. He was able to take this risk, and now I was, so I did. I gave him a copy of my plan, and he took it home with him.

A couple of days later, he came back and told me, "Joe, I think this is an absolutely outstanding idea. It's something the country needs, and it's something our community needs. It's a very large dream, but I think it can become a reality. However, there's a fatal flaw in the plan that you've laid out. You've got yourself acting as chairman of the executive committee, but you've got someone else in there acting as the chairman and chief executive of the entire operation. You've got someone else in there actually making it happen. You know, Joe, this is your dream, and if you're going to make it a reality, it's going to have to be you that does it. You've to be out there on the point, and you're going to have to devote 100 percent of your energy and 110 percent of your commitment to make it happen. And if you don't, you can just forget it. You're going to have to leave the law firm, quit the practice of law, and dedicate every ounce of energy and every minute of time that you have, or it just won't happen."

As the words were coming out of Tom's mouth, I knew that he was telling me the truth. What he was saying was absolutely correct, but I didn't have the guts to leave the practice of law and to take all of the attendant risks. I had promised my partners that I would go to London to open our new law office, and I used that as the excuse. I told Tom that the timing was wrong, and I simply couldn't do it.

He looked at me and said, "Whenever you're ready, let me know. I'm going to help you." In fact, a few years later, Tom was the person who gave me the crucial help I needed.

9. CAIRO

In early 1978, I moved to London to open our new law offices. The years over there unified my thinking in a way that would never have happened had I stayed in the States. I realized that the implications for the American Leadership Forum were global, that the free world looks to the United States as the model of democracy, and that if democracy is not working here, it's not going to work anywhere.

By 1979, commentators were writing about leadership in the United States. *Business Week, U.S. News & World Report, Newsweek*, and the leading newspapers were all carrying stories, and *Time* devoted a special issue (August 6, 1979) entirely to leadership, including a wonderful editorial by Lance Morrow entitled "A Cry for New Leadership: America Looks for Leaders Who Can Construct a New Consensus."

All of the writers addressed the same issues. They said there was a general retreat from community and national service all across the country, and that there was a self-absorption prevalent among the people of our generation, as well as a kind of a civic cynicism. They talked about the fact that demographic shifts had taken place in the country over the previous twenty years that had made it clear that the old style of community leadership and regional leadership would never be effective again. New attitudes and new kinds of leadership were necessary. We needed more open, flexible, and participatory kinds of leadership. The commentators were saying what John W. Gardner had said twenty years earlier: Communication among the diverse leadership elements—city hall, business, minorities—was the first condition for renewal in our communities and in our nation.

I was traveling all over Europe at this time, and whenever I could, I talked to high-level people in business and in government about what was happening in the world and in our own country. Perhaps living abroad brought a clearer understanding of the States. It's always that way when you walk away and see something from afar. What I saw was that people of my generation were self-absorbed and materialistic, bent on making more to get more. John Gardner had talked about the "anti-leadership vaccine" that we all received back in high school in the fifties and in college in the sixties. I don't recall one college professor or one mentor ever talking to me about leadership or about giving something back or about serving others. The focus was on picking a business or a profession, becoming preeminent in that field, and rising to the top.

I kept wondering what the key to all this really was. I couldn't put my finger on it, but I knew that this discussion all centered around *doing*, and although important, it was missing something crucial. It became clearer and clearer to me that the kind of leadership that could effect lasting change was centered around the *being* aspects of leadership.

I continued traveling and working and thinking about issues of leadership and what was happening in the States, but I didn't share my ideas with anyone.

In 1979, an opportunity arose for an association with a law firm in Cairo. Anthony Radcliff, an English lawyer who was a partner of mine in London, flew with me to Cairo. We spent about ten days there, and a lot of the time, instead of engaging in pure business, we visited in homes and went sightseeing, getting to know something about Egyptian culture and society.

Anthony and I spent a good deal of time alone, and I found myself talking with him about my dream of the American Leadership Forum. At that time I still didn't have a name for it. I was just describing the concept for him. I told him I felt that most of us were using only a fraction of the capacity that we really have. I longed to find a way to unlock that potential for constructive change in America and the world. I talked about Maslow's hierarchy of needs, and about how once we can get past satisfying our material desires, we can turn to satisfying our higher needs. I felt that there were five thousand or more people in the United States who, like me, had turned forty, having largely satisfied their needs for materialistic success, and who now wanted so much to live a life of meaning and adventure, but were simply afraid to take the first step. What they needed was some mechanism to nudge them, to connect them with others who were feeling the same way, and to heighten their sense of public responsibility. I told Anthony that I longed to help provide that mechanism for others because I knew deeply how badly it was needed. I was the prototype of the "successful" individual who had worked for years and years, making his mark in his profession, only to look up after twenty years and realize that he never had understood his true purpose for being here, and was not truly stepping into his real life. There was so much wasted talent around, so much hidden talent, and what I wanted to do was to help discover and develop that talent. I wanted to find a way of linking these people together into a national community of leaders who would develop the wisdom and the power to serve others. I envisioned a national, and later an international, community of servant leaders—a community of enlightened, committed people who could join hands in fact and in spirit and literally change their communities and the world—"the only thing that ever has," as Margaret Mead once said.

I told Anthony that I knew my idea sounded grandiose and perhaps a little naive, but that I deeply believed it. I believed I was being called to act as a catalyst to make all of this happen. I was almost ashamed to say it, but I felt I had the capacity to put this in place and help create a movement toward enlightened, committed, transformational leadership.

Anthony listened, and we talked back and forth over several days. He was a great listener and a very gentle person, almost coaxing the ideas out of me. It was not unlike what I had experienced speaking with Tom Fatjo several years before, when I had first had the dream but not the guts to step out and make it happen. Anthony inspired me simply by the way he listened. He made me know he expected great things from me.

><+>·O·<+><

Later, as I reflected on the conversations, it began dawning on me that Anthony was a true servant leader. He had my own interests at the center of his attention, and his questions and concern for me gave me a source of energy I had not received by any other means. I was struck by the fact that back in Steamboat Springs, the concept of servant leadership was at the center of my dream, and now I had experienced, in the most significant way, true servant leadership, the word made flesh.

><+>·O·<+><

Years later, when the American Leadership Forum was a reality, Anthony and I reminisced about our trip to Cairo. He told me that he had known then what was really not apparent to me—that I soon would be leaving the law firm to follow this dream. He never said a word about this to me in Cairo, but just continued to encourage me by listening to me describe the picture in my mind.

Leadership is all about the release of human possibilities. One of the central requirements for good leadership is the capacity to inspire the people in the group: to move them and encourage them and pull them into the activity, and to help them get centered and focused and operating at peak capacity. A key element of this capacity to inspire is communicating to people that you believe they matter, that you know they have something important to give. The confidence you have in others will to some degree determine the confidence they have in themselves. John Gardner put it succinctly:

> If one is leading, teaching, dealing with young people or engaged in any other activity that involves influencing, directing, guiding, helping or nurturing, the whole tone of the relationship is conditioned by one's faith in human possibilities. That is the generative element, the source of the current that gives life to the relationship.

Just being able to be there for others and to listen to them is one of the most important capacities a leader can have. It calls forth the best in people by allowing them to express what is within them. If someone listens to me say what I am feeling, then my feelings are given substance and direction, and I can act.

Anthony probably didn't agree with all that I was saying, but during the days in Cairo he listened intently, and I know he cared deeply. We would work and then go off and do something, and then come back to the hotel and talk. His listening allowed me to develop my thoughts. While I talked, his eyes never wandered. He looked directly at me and gave me his full attention, as if nothing else mattered in that moment. The more he listened, the more I was able to express myself and the more certain I became about what I was saying. This experience with Anthony taught me a great deal about the power of listening, about how fundamentally important it is in helping leaders dream and form their visions of the future.

As I talked to him about this back then, a great feeling of calm and peacefulness came over me. It felt right for me to be in this place, at this time, and to talk of this possibility.

Anthony's listening had something to do with it, and Cairo itself had something to do with it. I had spent quite a bit of time walking around by myself, and I felt I had actually been there before when, in fact, I had never visited Cairo. Yet as I walked in various places, I felt certain that I had seen them before. And I remember even taking a picture, which I have to this day, of a particular area that I felt connected to. It was a small open area in the heart of Cairo near a narrow walkway which eventually led to an ancient church. There was a place to sit and rest, and I found myself returning there again and again. The play of light there in the early morning and late afternoon fascinated me. Often when I was there, I would experience this strange ringing sound in my mind and would feel, without a shadow of a doubt, that I was fundamentally at one with the entire universe. My sense of identity expanded beyond me and embraced the entire world, the entire universe. This was a return of the same feeling I had experienced in the mountains, particularly when I had encountered the ermine, and it was the same feeling I had experienced at the great cathedral at Chartres. So I kept returning to this place in Cairo, and it became a kind of sacred place for me. My time there was quiet and very reflective and peaceful. I felt at one with myself and with the world.

10. COLLAPSING BOUNDARIES

My visit to Cairo was ended abruptly by a telephone call that I received at about five o'clock one morning. When I picked up the telephone, I heard my sister Joanie, who told me that she was over at my other sister's house and that she was calling to give me some terrible news: my nephew David had been killed in an automobile accident just a few hours earlier. She said that the whole family was gathered at Claire and Bob's house, and they were sitting around the telephone as they called me. I couldn't believe my ears, and I had a flashback to the time, just seven years earlier, when Joanie had called me with the same news about the death of her own son Mike. I was devastated, and I asked Joanie if I could talk to Claire.

When I got Claire on the phone, I could hardly talk. I just broke down, crying uncontrollably, and all I could utter between sobs was "I'm so sorry, I'm so sorry, I'm so sorry." Claire was trying to help me, as crazy as it sounds, but that's the way it sometimes works at times like this. She was trying to comfort me, but I was helpless.

Joanie had previously told me that nothing—not the loss of a parent, or of a spouse, or even the impending loss of your own life—compares to the pain of losing one of your own children. I was feeling Claire's pain at the loss of her son, and I completely broke apart. It was as if there was, at that moment, a complete and total connection between Claire and me. Our emotions were one. I was crying her tears; there was but one tear. It was as if time and space had disappeared, and Claire and I were the same person, as if I had merged at that moment, at that instant with her. There was something terrifying about that experience.

I don't recall much of what happened during that conversation, but looking back, I now realize that I had experienced another collapse of boundaries similar to those experienced earlier, but this time the disappearance of the boundaries was so complete and involved such pain that it left another indelible mark on me.

As I flew back home, I thought about all of this. I had experienced in a short time such strong feelings of euphoria and oneness with the world, and suddenly the deepest and most profound pain and oneness with Claire. On the plane I was trying to make sense out of what had happened. I was unable to articulate it, but at a deep level I knew I had to find a way to understand this dynamic, this opening up to the world. Somehow I knew it was part of my journey.

When I finally got into Houston, it was the day of the funeral. The service was conducted by a very close friend of Claire's, Bob's, and mine, the Reverend Robert Ball of the Memorial Drive Presbyterian Church. It was Bob Ball who had helped sustain me during the darkest days of my divorce. It was a wonderful service. Instead of making it a morbid affair, Bob made it more like a celebration of David's life. Robert and John, David's brothers, gave beautiful testimonials to David. And then Bob spoke. He talked about David's way of living his life: to the fullest and highly independently. He did things his own way and expected others to do the same.

As Dr. Ball spoke of David, he called him "Eli," a nickname his close friends had given him. "Last night," Dr. Ball said during the course of his remarks, "it came to me how uniquely rare it is to have contact with another human being, one who truly treats you as an equal. Eli did that for me. These moments are so precious, so full of life, they are so much of what life at its best is meant to be, that when they are happening to you, you have the impulse to take off your shoes, for you are standing on holy ground." Later in his remarks Dr. Ball mentioned that human life, according to the scriptures, is not a matter of having arrived somewhere, but it's a matter of being on the road, being on the way, a matter of becoming. He said "Somehow, some way, the message had gotten through to Eli that life is a place to be lived, and so he continually took it out into the marketplace and lived it. The life that Eli lived was full of meaning.

"I don't have the explanation for why tragedies such as this occur," said Dr. Ball. "I cannot claim any special wisdom as to how it is all going to turn out. But it's my hunch that Eli, who treated me and a lot of other human beings as equals, was right at the center of what it's all about, and still is and always will be."

We buried David next to Joanie's son Mike. At the burial services, as I was looking at the casket covered with flowers, I felt a strong closeness and presence with David. After the burial service was concluded, and we were walking away toward our cars, I had the impulse to pause and take a final look at the flower-covered casket. As I fixed my eyes on the casket, I could swear that I saw David sitting on top of that casket. His arms were folded, and he had that slight smile on his face that I remember so often. His eyes were looking directly at mine, and his head was cocked slightly to the side. In a firm voice, he said, "Go for it!" I know it must have been my imagination, but I can see it as clearly now as I did then.

It was as if David was giving me that final blessing, that final nudge or permission to leave everything behind, acknowledging how deeply the events of the past two weeks had affected me.

I turned and continued walking toward the car. Even to this day, I don't fully understand it, but at that point I *knew* my journey had begun.

PART TWO

CROSSING THE THRESHOLD

⊱—◦—⊰

There was a dizzy, sickening sensation of sight
that was not like seeing; I saw Line that was no Line;
Space that was not Space. I was myself and not myself.
When I could find voice, I shrieked aloud
in agony, "Either this is madness or it is Hell."
"It is neither," calmly replied the voice of the Sphere.
"It is Knowledge; it is Three Dimensions.
Open your eyes once again and try to look steadily."

—Edwin A. Abbott, *Flatland*

11. THE MYSTERY OF COMMITMENT

After David's funeral, I flew to New York to talk to Bernadette. I felt she was the kind of friend I needed at this time—someone who could understand at a deep level the inner struggle I had been having over the past few years.

I had not seen Bernadette since that Sunday morning in Cannes back in 1976, but when I had returned to Houston then, I had found a small package waiting for me. It bore a return address of the small hotel in Paris where Bernadette had stayed those few days during her meeting there. In it was a paperback book carefully covered in beautiful wrapping paper so as to make a new jacket. The book was *Demian*, by Herman Hesse. There was an inscription on the inside cover from Bernadette, and only one page had been marked by turning the edge of the page down. The passage read:

> Each man had only one genuine vocation—to find the way to himself. . . .
> His task was to discover his own destiny—not an arbitrary one—and live it
> out wholly and resolutely within himself. Everything else was only a would-
> be existence, an attempt at evasion, a flight back to the ideals of the
> masses, conformity and fear of one's own inwardness.

Over the ensuing years I had often turned back to that passage and the story of Emil Sinclair's youth, a classic document of the most ancient of all quests—the search for self-knowledge. In New York, Bernadette and I spent a day talking together about the apprehension and anxiety I felt over the step I was contemplating. Bernadette, like Anthony, was helping me to see more clearly the path I was choosing to take.

From New York I went back to London, thought for several weeks, and finally made the toughest decision I've ever made in my life: to resign from the law firm, to leave the partners and colleagues and friends who had been such a big part of my life for so many years. Leaving these people was like leaving members of my own family. I had spent twenty years at the firm by that time, and it was tough to break away. At first they tried to dissuade me from leaving. Then when it appeared that I was going and that nothing could stop me, the mood changed. It was more like a divorce. I think they felt rejected, and I felt misunderstood. They thought I was crazy to walk away from a successful law practice to do something that no one could really understand. I couldn't blame them. I didn't share a whole lot of the dream with them because I felt embarrassed to do so. I didn't think they would fully understand—I didn't even fully understand at that point, so how could they? I heard a lot of talk about the fact that "Joe's gone off the deep end." In a way, I guess I had. I felt very different and removed from my peers and colleagues. I felt just as if I were going on a long journey, and it would be quite a while, if ever, until I would return to be with them. I walked off into my own world.

I realize now that for at least a couple of years I had been growing more and more apart from the world of my life before my journey began, and nearer and nearer to this different person who was on a journey. Part of this was wrestling with my fearfulness and denial of my capacity to make a real difference in the world—the "Who, me?" syndrome. I had found so many ways over the years in London to rationalize how important my busy life was. "I'm up to my eyeballs in building the law firm. Anyway, how could I ever get my arms around building better leadership for the country?" I kept denying my destiny because of my insecurity, my dread of ostracism, my anxiety, and my lack of courage to risk myself. I was yielding to the pressure I felt within myself to conform to my peer group. Somewhere, deep down, I knew that to cooperate with destiny would bring great responsibility, and I was too fearful to accept that responsibility. I realize now that I was being called to engage my destiny, and by doing so, as Joseph Campbell says, I would be yielding to the design of the universe, which was speaking through the design of my own person. But I was unwilling to make the supreme effort that called for.

In Houston, when I felt called to fulfill my dream and shared it with Tom Fatjo, I ultimately filed it in "the box labeled 'too hard.'" I couldn't get past the fear of the unknown and the material sacrifice I would have to make. I was fixed in my cocoon of security and remained, in large part, in the sphere of the comfort of familiar people—my own tribe, so to speak.

Yet, on another plane, I was spending more and more time alone, writing and reading and thinking and reflecting and meditating. This is what I did with my evenings and my weekends. Every spare moment was engaged in the inner struggle, thinking about the new forum, seeing pictures of it in my mind, pictures of how it would be, and pictures of the results. Over time, the pictures of the new enterprise became all-consuming. This vision began to pervade every part of me. I became it and it became me, and it was to be that way for the next ten years.

At the moment of decision, it was as if I had no real choice. It was not so much a decision about what I "ought" to do—rather, I could not do otherwise. At this moment, says Rollo May, one arrives at a point where freedom and destiny merge. It was at this point that my words became action.

In London, I began selling everything that I had, all the material goods and the trappings that I had accumulated—my DB5, my BMW, my flat in Chelsea. I guess that I was getting ready for the journey, getting ready to travel light.

My last evening at work, my English colleagues had a little cocktail party for me. It seemed that they were more accepting and understood what it was all about more than my American partners did. I think it was because in many ways my American partners and I had grown up together. They knew the old Joe and had not gotten to know the new Joe. My English colleagues had been with me for the entire three years, and although I didn't realize it at the time, I think they saw this growing within me. At any rate, the evening I walked away from that going-away party was when I knew my commitment was firm. There was no turning back. This was it.

At the moment I walked away from the firm, a strange thing happened. I clearly had no earthly idea how I would proceed. I knew next to nothing about leadership curriculum and development. I knew no one who could help me on the substantive side of things, no network of experts. The resources necessary for a national effort would be enormous, far exceeding my own capacity. I had none of this, only myself. Yet, at that point, strangely enough, most of my concerns and doubts about the enormity of the project were erased. I had a great sense of internal direction and focus, and an incredible sense of freedom that I had never felt before in my entire life. I had committed to something far larger than myself—and through that step, as I was to realize over time, I would achieve a quality of meaning and adventure I had never before attained.

As I had no specific knowledge, only the guidance of the dream I had formed during the two weeks in Steamboat Springs, I made up my mind to take one day at a time, one step at a time. There was an inner confidence that things would work out in the right way. This was a kind of commitment that was not entirely new to me. I had experienced some of these same feelings as I had stepped out to help form the insurance company and the Alaskan refinery and in building the law firm. But in each of those instances, there was a group of us, and we had among us the experience and expertise on which to build our confidence. In this instance, I was alone without any expertise or experience whatsoever. All I had was my dream and my inner resources.

Paradoxically, at this moment I had the feeling of certainty that I *would* accomplish this dream. I felt nothing could deter me; I would not let anything get in my way. Looking back, I was so single-minded at times that I unknowingly offended a lot of people, including some in my family, very close loved ones, and members of my firm. I feel badly about that now, and hope that I've learned a valuable lesson from that. But I had a highly focused commitment that continued to drive me forward. As I look back on it, it was almost irrational, because the dream was so large.

The day I left the firm, I crossed the threshold. From that point on, what happened to me had the most mysterious quality about it. Things began falling into place almost effortlessly—unforeseen incidents and meetings with the most remarkable people who were to provide crucial assistance to me.

12. THE GUIDE

It was Sunday, July 27, 1980. I had resigned from the law firm the week before and was spending day and night writing, thinking, and struggling with the philosophical underpinnings of the new enterprise I had decided to found, especially the new leadership curriculum that would be its foundation.

That day, I got up before dawn and went for a long, slow, easy run in Hyde Park. When I returned, I picked up the *Sunday Times* and went into my flat. After showering, I was thumbing through the newspaper, and when I got to page fourteen, I saw a headline in the education section: "How the Universe Hangs Together." There was a picture of Dr. David Bohm, Professor of Theoretical Physics at London's Birkbeck College, with a caption underneath: "Bohm and his algebra of algebras: 'religion is wholeness.'" I knew at that moment that this was speaking to me.

I threw the rest of the paper on the floor and read every word of the article about Dr. Bohm. It began by saying that he was soon to publish a revolutionary scientific theory that might at last bring unity to the world of modern physics. "For the first time since the comfortable certitudes of classical physics were shattered—in contradictory ways—by Einstein's theory of relativity and by quantum theory, there is hope that physicists' disparate views of reality may be understood in a unified way."

The article described the new theory, referring to Bohm's latest book, *Wholeness and the Implicate Order*. It described Bohm as a friend and colleague of Einstein's at Princeton in the forties and fifties, and said he was now one of the most eminent living physicists. Bohm had written two classical works on quantum theory and made significant contributions to plasma physics. The article said that it had been Bohm's passion, in both his life and his work, to find some unifying concept in physics that could help heal the fragmentation in physics and society. For the past twenty years, Bohm had devoted himself to formulating a general theory that would get beyond the contradictions posed by relativity theory and quantum theory.

Bohm's theory of the implicate order was highly technical. I didn't understand a lot of what was said in the article, but at another level, I understood it all. It was the answer that I was searching for. I suddenly felt I had to meet this person. The article continued: ". . . the theory also has deeply important philosophical implications, about which Bohm writes at great length in his book. It provides a world view that gives a coherent understanding of physical phenomena, and it suggests that both the material world and consciousness are parts of a single unbroken totality of movement." The article went on:

> Bohm's work on non-locality and his wedding of physics and consciousness have caused some para-psychologists to look to his theory for an explanation of such phenomena as telepathy, precognition and psycho-kinesis. Bohm is not hostile to this, but maintains firm neutrality.

> The Implicate Order (from the Latin "to be enfolded") is a level of reality beyond our normal everyday thoughts and perceptions, as well as beyond any picture of reality offered by a given scientific theory. These, according to Bohm, belong to "the explicit order."

> In the Implicate Order, the totality of existence is enfolded within each "fragment" of space and time—whether it be a single object, thought or event. Thus everything in the universe affects everything else because they are all part of the same unbroken whole.

> Bohm thinks that the current trend towards fragmentation is embedded in the subject-verb-object structure of our grammar, and is reflected at the personal and social levels by our tendency to see individuals and groups as "other" than ourselves, leading to isolation, selfishness and wars.

Bingo. This was it. This was what I'd been feeling and dreaming and thinking about. It was a way of expressing the fundamental basis of our leadership curriculum. It provided the framework for the optimism that I was feeling: that our country could exert moral, transformational leadership if we could only see the world as it really is, in all of its intricate design.

I went to the telephone and began dialing. After several calls, I found Bohm's home number, and before I knew it, he was at the other end of the line. I was pouring my heart out, telling him what I was about and that I must see him. Almost without hesitation, he agreed to spend the entire next afternoon with me.

This was another of the many predictable miracles that I was to experience as this adventure unfolded. The next day, I was in Bohm's office and spent over four hours with him, tape-recording our conversation.

We talked about the marriage of the principles of physics and philosophy and its relevance for my dream of the Leadership Forum. He raised questions with me that are both ancient and fundamental. What is mind? What is matter? What is the source of the simple symmetry we see all around us in the natural world? He told me that the old concepts of time, space, and matter no longer apply. We talked about life in the "bubble chamber," where physicists look at matter and examine particles at a sub-atomic level. On that level, matter is sometimes a particle and sometimes a wave. Matter is constantly in motion. The picture of a rock or a board or a piece of steel as solid matter does not comport with reality. Particles also sometimes move backward in time. In the bubble chamber, notions of earlier and later are no longer clear. Time-space processes sometimes run in reverse causal sequences.

We talked about Bell's theorem, which was my introduction to the oneness of the sub-atomic world. Bell's theorem was proposed in 1964 by J. S. Bell, a Swiss physicist and former student of Bohm's. It was confirmed experimentally eight years later by the physicist Alain Aspect at the University of Paris. In his 1975 government-sponsored report, physicist Henry Stapp of the University of California at Berkeley said that Bell's theorem is "the most profound discovery in the history of science." It proves, in effect, that the world is fundamentally inseparable.

The simplest explanation I can give of Bell's theorem is this: Imagine two paired particles in a two-particle system. If you make them fly apart or take them apart any distance—putting one particle in New York, say, and another in San Francisco—then, if you change the spin of one of these particles, the other particle will simultaneously change its own spin. The effect is a simple consequence of the oneness of apparently separate objects. It is a quantum loophole through which physics admits the necessity of a unitary vision. As Bohm said, "We are all one."

Bohm told me about the general implications of Bell's theorem. He said the world view of modern physics is now a systems view. Everything is connected to everything else. We are not sure how this connectedness works, but there is a certainty that there is "separation without separateness." That is the way our universe is constructed. "The oneness implicit in Bell's theorem envelops human beings and atoms alike."

Bohm's conversation with me was like a bolt of lightning. On the one hand, I felt that I knew this at a deep level and had known it all along. At another level, I felt a fear of knowing. There was a responsibility inherent in this new knowledge. We were talking about a radical, disorienting new view of reality which we couldn't ignore. We were talking about the awareness of the essential interrelatedness and interdependence of all phenomena—physiological, social, and cultural. We were talking about a systems view of life and a systems view of the universe. Nothing could be understood in isolation, everything had to be seen as a part of the unified whole. It is an abstraction, Bohm said, to talk of nonliving matter. Different people are not that separate, they are all enfolded into the whole, and they are all a manifestation of the whole. It is only through an abstraction that they look separate. Everything is included in everything else.

"You cannot think of existence as local," Bohm said to me that afternoon. To illustrate, he told me of a simple experiment using a device with two glass concentric cylinders, one fixed and one turning slowly. You put a highly viscous fluid such as glycerin between the cylinders, and you put an insoluble drop of ink in the fluid. As you turn the outer cylinder, the drop of ink gets drawn into a thin thread because the outer cylinder is going faster than the inner cylinder. As the ink particles get farther and farther apart, the ink ultimately becomes invisible. Now comes the amazing part. If you reverse the motion and turn the outer cylinder backward, the ink droplet becomes visible again.

While the ink droplet was invisible, Bohm said, "it still had an order, but it was enfolded into the glycerin. Physics is suggesting that that order is very significant." So, "Instead of thinking of a particle as a single solid object," he added, "we can think of it as a series of droplets, enfolded at different numbers of turns. Seen this way, we can say that matter basically has its existence in the whole and manifests in a localized way rather than saying that its fundamental existence is made up of separate parts."

He said, "Yourself is actually the whole of mankind. That's the idea of implicate order—that everything is enfolded in everything. The entire past is enfolded in each one of us in a very subtle way. If you reach deeply into yourself, you are reaching into the very essence of mankind. When you do this, you will be led into the generating depth of consciousness that is common to the whole of mankind and that has the whole of mankind enfolded in it. The individual's ability to be sensitive to that becomes the key to the change of mankind. We are all connected. If this could be taught, and if people could understand it, we would have a different consciousness.

"At present, people create barriers between each other by their fragmentary thought. Each one operates separately. When these barriers have dissolved, then there arises one mind, where they are all one unit, but each person also retains his or her own individual awareness. That one mind will still exist even when they separate, and when they come together, it will be as if they hadn't separated. It's actually a single intelligence that works with people who are moving in relationship with one another. Cues that pass from one to the other are being picked up with the same awareness, just as we pick up cues in riding bicycles or skiing. Therefore, these people are really all one. The separation between them is not blocking. They are all pulling together. If you had a number of people who really pulled together and worked together in this way, it would be remarkable. They would stand out so much that everyone would know they were different.

"There is a difficulty with only one person changing," said Bohm. "People call that person a great saint or a great mystic or a great leader, and they say, 'Well, he's different from me—I could never do it.' What's wrong with most people is that they have this block—they feel they could never make a difference, and therefore, they never face the possibility, because it is too disturbing, too frightening."

At this point I told Bohm a story about an extraordinary experience I had had a number of years before. A friend had invited me to go skeet shooting while I visited him in Georgia. I had not used a shotgun for about ten years, so early that morning I went out for a run, then came back and sat still and pictured myself shooting in the perfect way. As soon as I finished meditating, my friend came by to pick me up to go to the skeet range.

In skeet shooting, twenty-five targets comprise the usual round. A highly accomplished skeet shooter might hit twenty-three out of twenty-five targets, so hitting twelve targets in itself is a pretty good score for a novice like me. We started going from station to station, and by the time we came to number twelve, I had hit all twelve of the targets. A few people gathered around to watch. I hit target after target—fourteen, eighteen, twenty. . . . At the twenty-fifth target I was still in the flow state and was totally peaceful. By this time, there were quite a few onlookers. Then someone turned to me and said, "You realize you've got one more to shoot a perfect score." At that point, I started trying, and I missed.

I learned from this and other experiences that the mind has powers that allow us to go beyond our normal or habitual way of being, and beyond what we think is possible. When people join together and go beyond their habitual way of being as a group, even more possibilities open up. But somehow a kind of block prevents these extraordinary experiences from happening.

Bohm said, "You've got to give attention to that block. You've got to find out where it comes from both in yourself and in anybody. If you were able to get a group of people working together with one another at a different plane, they might find a new way to operate that would not be simply individual. A new individual arises which is the whole concept, you see? The individuals would operate as if with one mind. If the results were in the domain of public knowledge, public experience, then people couldn't explain it away. If such a group got beyond a certain point, it could have a real impact."

Bohm then told me, "You've got to give a lot of attention to consciousness. This is one of the things of which our society is ignorant. It assumes consciousness requires no attention. But consciousness is what gives attention. Consciousness itself requires very alert attention or else it will simply destroy itself. It's a very delicate mechanism.

"We have to think with everything we have. We have to think with our muscles. We have to think, as Einstein said, with feelings in our muscles. Think with everything. And so it is a flowing process which also goes outward and inward and makes communication possible."

Even as he spoke, I thought about the way I was able to communicate with the ermine. I thought about meeting Manny Deitz and Bernadette and the language of the eyes.

Bohm then told me that we have capacities within us that we do not recognize. "For example, when you ride a bicycle, you are engaging in a movement you can't describe or even comprehend. That's the implicate order that is enfolded in you. You have capacities within you that are phenomenal, if you only knew how to release them."

As we were walking out, Bohm gave me some advice. He said, "You're on the verge of a creative movement. Just go with it. You cannot be fixed in how you're going about it any more than you would be fixed if you were setting about to paint a great work of art. Be alert, be self-aware, so that when opportunity presents itself, you can actually rise to it."

When I left Bohm's office, my mind was reeling. I knew I had been in the presence of greatness and that it would take a lifetime to fully understand what Bohm had said. It had truly been a life-changing experience for me. More immediately, the fundamental precept for the Leadership Forum had been validated. It was my feeling all along that a number of committed people could literally change the world. I realized now that this was not just an idle dream or unwarranted optimism, but a principle I could hang my hat on because it was consistent with the laws of natural order.

During our conversation, Bohm had emphasized as an essential feature of modern physics that all things were in sympathy. He mentioned Mach's principle: "The whole is as necessary to the understanding of its parts, as the parts are necessary to the understanding of the whole." I felt the implications of this were profound. The universe as a whole influences local events. Local events have an influence, however small, on the universe as a whole. I recalled the Chinese proverb, "If you cut a blade of grass, you shake the universe."

When we parted, Bohm's final words to me were, "Everything starts with you and me." As I walked away, I knew I would have to find a way for the Leadership Forum to give its fellows an "inner education" so that they would identify themselves with all humanity. If they could do that, they could literally help change the world.

13. SYNCHRONICITY:
THE CUBIC CENTIMETER OF CHANCE

All of us, whether or not we are warriors, have a cubic centimeter of
chance that pops out in front of our eyes from time to time.
The difference between an average man and a warrior is that the warrior
is aware of this, and one of his tasks is to be alert, deliberately waiting,
so that when his cubic centimeter pops out he has the necessary speed,
the prowess, to pick it up.

—Carlos Castaneda

A couple of months after meeting Bohm, I took a trip to the States with my son to visit colleges and universities that he was interested in attending. We were in O'Hare Airport, running down one of the crowded aisleways in an effort to catch a plane that was about to leave. Joey and I were running two abreast, dodging our way through the crowd. Up ahead, I noticed a very beautiful young woman walking quickly toward us. As I came within a few feet of her, I looked into her eyes, which were absolutely gorgeous. I stopped dead in my tracks, and as she passed me, I turned around and said to myself, "I've got to go get her. I know her from somewhere." I was absolutely dumbstruck. It was very mysterious, almost as if (to paraphrase something Joseph Campbell once said) the future life I was going to have with her had already been told to me. It was something talking to me from what was to be. It had to do with the mystery and transcendence of time.

As she walked away, I just stood there, looking back in her direction. Joey had run far up ahead and when he noticed I was not there, he came running back to me and pulled at my arm. "My God, Dad, what are you doing? We're about to miss the plane. Come on!" I turned around to Joey and remembering an old John Wayne line I said, "Joey, there comes a time when a man's gotta do what a man's gotta do. You go ahead and catch the plane. I'll catch the next one. I'll find you some way." As I think about it now, this was probably the most irresponsible thing a father could have done under such circumstances. But at that moment I was acting on instinct, and there was not a trace of guilt within me.

Without another word, I turned around and started running after the woman. I found her at an American Airlines gate, just about to board a plane for Dallas. I ran up to her as she was giving her ticket to the gate agent and pulled her back. I said, "Pardon me, but I have to talk to you. Please come over here." The woman took a step away from the entrance to the ramp, and before she could say anything, I said "Tell me, are you married?"

She looked at me and said "No, are you?"

Somewhat flustered, I said "Well, of course not, but look, I live in London, and I know we've never met, but I feel that I know you from someplace. I need to get your name and telephone number so I can contact you."

The woman looked at me and without another word pulled out one of her cards and wrote her home number on it and gave it to me and said, "I'd love to learn more about London."

Her flight was closing out, so with that, she boarded the plane. I stood there for a few moments and then turned around and realized that Joey had been standing nearby, watching the whole affair. As we ran to catch our plane, I was trying to explain to him what happened, but I couldn't.

Late that night, we arrived at our motel. It was one o'clock in the morning when I noted in my journal: "I met a woman by the name of Mavis Webster today at O'Hare Airport. She was very beautiful, and I was only with her for two or three minutes before she boarded her plane, but I have the strangest feeling. In her presence I felt this warmth. When my eyes met hers, it was a spiritual thing. When I ran after her, it was as if nothing else mattered. I can hardly describe any of this. It is very mysterious. But it feels like love."

For some reason or another I didn't see that passage again until over a year later, when Mavis and I were already married. I don't even remember writing it in my journal, but there it is, in black and white.

Mavis was the producer and the on-camera talent for an evening television show in a town near Dallas. She had been invited by an ABC affiliate in Chicago to interview for a similar job in that market. The night before she left for Chicago, she had a dream and a strong premonition about meeting a man who would become a significant part of her life. After she had concluded her business and while she was in Chicago, she visited a number of friends and went to two parties. Each time she would meet a man, she wondered whether he was the one, but he never seemed to materialize. Her last night in Chicago, just before she left for the airport, she told her girlfriend about this dream, and how disappointed she was that it had not materialized. It was the next morning that I grabbed her arm just as she was about to board the airplane.

When I moved to Houston to begin organizing the Leadership Forum, I called her and made no fewer than five dates with her. She had to break all five of them due to the press of her business. The sixth time I called her I said, "Mavis, this is Joseph. I want to ask you to have lunch with me in Dallas. If you break the date with me, I'll understand that you really don't want to be with me. I'll never call you again." She explained earnestly that it was the nature of her business that had caused all of this inconvenience, and she assured me that she wanted to be with me again.

We met about two weeks later for lunch in Dallas. It was magical. We spent the rest of that day talking about our hopes and our dreams for the world. She spoke of her dream to become a doctor, to care for and heal the sick, and ultimately to be able to do missionary work in various parts of the world. And I spoke of my hopes and dreams for the American Leadership Forum and how it might make a difference to communities not only in the United States but, ultimately, throughout the world. We spoke of the mystery surrounding the way that we met, and of Mavis's gifts of acute perception and intuition. We went to walk in a beautiful park in central Dallas, and the more we were together, and the more we talked, the more we both had a feeling of ecstasy as the boundaries between us became blurred and thin. We identified not only with one another but with all the world.

We went out to dinner that night and spent much of the next day together. Mavis helped me to see much more about the fundamental truths I had recently learned, and I committed to help her in every way I could to become a physician and fulfill her dream. Mavis moved to Houston, and we were married a little over a year later.

It was a wonderfully simple, but beautiful ceremony, a family affair held at the Chapel of the Presbyterian Church where our good friend Bob Ball was pastor. Joey was my best man, and my sister Claire was Mavis's matron of honor. This was but the necessary formality; I had felt totally connected with Mavis from that first magical day in Dallas.

In the interim, Mavis had traveled with me as I assembled the Board of Trustees and began building the curriculum for the program. She stuck with me and supported me and helped me every step of the way. Her love for me was genuine love, which implied a lifetime commitment to extend herself for the purpose of nurturing me, my spiritual growth, and my dream. That's what she committed to do and that's what she's done. I felt a deep need to make the same kind of commitment to her, and I pray every day that I will have the strength to fulfill that commitment.

M. Scott Peck compares marriage to a base camp for mountain climbing. If you want to make a peak climb, you've got to have a good base camp, a place where there is shelter and where provisions are kept, where one may receive nurture and rest before one ventures forth again to seek another summit. "Successful mountain climbers know that they must spend at least as much time, if not more, in tending to their base camp as they actually do in climbing mountains, for their survival is dependent upon their seeing to it that their base camp is sturdily constructed and well stocked."

I've learned a lot about tending base camp while Mavis has been working her way through medical school, internship, and now residency; and I've learned a lot about the value of both of us tending to one another and both venturing forth. But I've had a hard time learning this, because my tendency is to focus completely on the task at hand, almost to the exclusion of everything else. I made this mistake in my first marriage, and I've now experienced the value of balance in a marital relationship, where both male and female tend the hearth, and both venture forth. I still have a lot to learn, but I feel that this is truly the way.

>-+>-0-<+-+-<

I've thought a great deal about the way both Bohm and Mavis showed up in my life right after I made the commitment to leave the firm and follow my dream. At the time, I was amazed by the coincidence of it all. But when I thought about it, particularly in light of what Bohm had taught me, I told myself, "Why be surprised? This is the way things should work in a world that is fundamentally connected." Yet all my old conditioning made me see the world as fragmented, as made up of separate "things," so I continually struggled to find a reason to connect "things" together. It was difficult for me to consistently see the world as one of relatedness rather than thingness.

In this process, I began reading all I could about synchronicity, beginning with C. G. Jung's classic work, "Synchronicity: An Acausal Connecting Principle." Jung defines "synchronicity" as "a meaningful coincidence of two or more events, where something other than the probability of chance is involved." At the very moment when we are struggling to attain a sense of personal autonomy, we are also caught up in vital forces that are larger than ourselves, so that while we may be protagonists of our own lives, we are important participants in a larger drama.

I also found Arthur Koestler's account of synchronicity in *Janus* helpful. Koestler traces the idea of unity-in-diversity all the way back to the Pythagorean harmony of the spheres and the Hippocratics' "sympathy of all things"—"There is one common flow, one common breathing, all things are in sympathy." The doctrine that everything in the universe hangs together also runs as a leitmotif through the teachings of Taoism, Buddhism, the Neo-Platonists, and the philosophers of the early Renaissance. Koestler concluded that "telepathy, clairvoyance, precognition . . . and synchronicity are merely different manifestations under different conditions of the same universal principle—i.e., the integrative tendency operating through both causal and acausal agencies."

I felt that at this time of my life I was working in the flow of things, in accord with the natural unfolding of the whole system, and so I would just continue to move in that way. I kept always in the forefront of my mind Bohm's injunction:

> Just go with it. You cannot be fixed in how you're going about it any more than you would be fixed if you were setting about to paint a great work of art. Be alert, be self-aware, so that when opportunity presents itself, you can actually rise to it.

I've never received better advice in my life. As I was to discover, acting in the belief that I was part of a greater whole while maintaining flexibility, patience, and acute awareness led to "all manner of unforeseen incidents and meetings and material assistance which no man could have dreamed would have come his way."

PART THREE

THE HERO'S JOURNEY

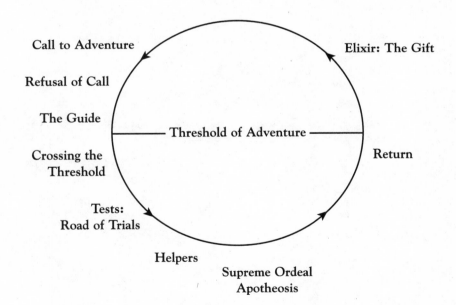

Call to Adventure

Refusal of Call

The Guide

Threshold of Adventure

Crossing the
Threshold

Return

Tests:
Road of Trials

Elixir: The Gift

Helpers

Supreme Ordeal
Apotheosis

Adapted from Joseph Campbell, *The Hero with a Thousand Faces*.

14. THE MOMENT OF SWING

One day in London, after my meeting with David Bohm, I was walking down the street pondering the most pressing issue facing me: How would I find the necessary expert help to construct the curriculum for the Leadership Forum? I knew next to nothing about building such a curriculum—it was a field completely alien to me. Bohm and I had talked about the need to develop a truly extraordinary kind of educational experience for the Forum fellows. The program needed to be designed to take the fellows on a year-long journey toward wholeness—thinking whole and being whole. We were talking about fundamental shifts of mind and being. It was, to say the least, a tall order.

To this day, I don't know what caused me to stop and pick up the magazine out of the news rack, but I did. I picked up a *U.S. News & World Report* and there staring me in the face was a caption on the cover "RX for Leadership in America." I opened the magazine and found the article by Tom Cronin. On the two pages in front of me the author had laid out a number of the principles that I had been thinking about. It was clear that Cronin was aligned with the concept of the Leadership Forum. I bought the magazine, tore the pages out, and flew to the States to find Cronin at Colorado College near Colorado Springs. Within a couple of days, I was at his home telling him about my dream. He listened intently for an hour and a half. At the end he said, "You can count on me. Sign me up. I'll be your first trustee. Now the first person you've got to go see is John W. Gardner. He's probably the most experienced person in the country in this particular field."

Gardner was the founder of the White House Fellows Program, the model I had in mind when I was creating my vision for the Leadership Forum. He was one of the most highly respected educators in the land and the author of *Self-Renewal*, a book which spoke to the very heart and spirit of the kind of program I envisioned. He had served six presidents of the United States in various leadership capacities. He had been Secretary of Health, Education, and Welfare (HEW), Chairman of the National Coalition, founding Chairman of Common Cause, and President of the Carnegie Corporation.

I looked at Tom and said, "I've read just about everything Gardner has written, and I know that he would be a crucial addition to the team—but I don't think I could get in his front door." Cronin said that he had been in the first class of White House Fellows and was Gardner's aide while he served as Secretary of HEW. He picked up the telephone and made an appointment for me. Within two days, I found myself walking into Gardner's office.

Gardner was formal, almost stoic. He greeted me, and as I sat down across the desk from him, he said "What can I do for you?" I began telling him about my dream and what I had in mind. I finished by telling him that what I envisioned was larger in scope than discovering and developing leadership for our country. I told him that I thought the world was on the threshold of a golden era, and that what we did as citizens of this planet would determine whether we would make it, that we were truly at a turning point, and that American leaders could play a pivotal role in the human race making this transition.

When I finished, Gardner sat there and looked at me for a few moments. For the first time in our meeting, I felt that perhaps I had dropped the ball, or said something that had turned him off, because he sat there and looked at me for the longest time. Then without saying a word, he turned around in his chair and shuffled through some papers. When he found what he was looking for, he turned around and thrust some papers in front of me and said, "Here, read this." It was an eight-page letter that Gardner had written to Joe Slater, head of the Aspen Institute. It was the most beautifully written letter I had ever seen; it read like a finely crafted essay. In essence it stated the basic points that I had just been making to Gardner. I looked up, and he was smiling. He said, "So you can see, Mr. Jaworski, I agree with what you are saying, and I want to help you." Then he looked me straight in the eye and said, "Are you serious about this? Are you serious about dedicating yourself to this?"

I told him that I had just left my law firm and reiterated the whole story to him. When I finished, he said, "Look, I'm in the process of getting off boards in order to devote my time to writing on the subject of leadership." He had just resigned from the boards of Shell Oil Company and the New York Telephone Company, among others. "What you are about is of great interest to me and is of great importance to the country and the world." He said he would sign on, and he would help guide me along the way. He said the next person I had to meet was Harlan Cleveland, former Ambassador to NATO, former President of the University of Hawaii, and one of the most knowledgeable thinkers and practitioners of leadership in the world today. He said that Cleveland had just been appointed Dean of the Humphrey Institute of Public Affairs at the University of Minnesota. He made an appointment for me to see Cleveland, and I was off to Minneapolis that evening.

Cleveland signed on and became Chairman of our Program Committee. He led me to James MacGregor Burns, the Pulitzer Prize-winning historian and preeminent scholar on leadership. Burns had just finished writing what many consider one of the seminal works on leadership. I went to see him, and he warmly embraced the project and signed on. He led me to Warren Bennis of the University of Southern California, who led me to Rosabeth Moss Kantor, then of Yale and now Harvard, and to Mayor Tom Bradley of Los Angeles. They all signed on. Then I went to see Michael Macoby, who was Eric Fromm's protégé, and who was gaining quite a reputation for his excellent books on business leadership. Gardner had also led me to Elsa Porter, former Assistant Secretary for Administration in the U.S. Department of Commerce and one of the most outstanding practitioners and thinkers on the subject of women in leadership in the country. I then went to see Admiral James Bond Stockdale who was one of the foremost authorities on military leadership, now teaching at Stanford University. They all agreed to serve.

It was a beautiful odyssey, and by the time it was over, I had signed up seventeen world-class thinkers, scholars, and practitioners of leadership—people who could, together, construct the kind of curriculum I was dreaming about.

In the midst of all this early organizational work, Mavis and I were married. In May 1981, we were near San Francisco on our honeymoon. I had recently read an exciting article by Willis Harman of the Stanford Research Institute in Palo Alto. One day, during a drive out into the wine country, I turned to Mavis and said, "Honey, I keep feeling I need to have a meeting with this man Willis Harman. I hate to do business during the honeymoon, but I can't get this off my mind. I've got to call him." As it turned out, my apprehension was completely misplaced. When I told Mavis about Harman, she was as excited about meeting him as I was.

Later that night, I found Harman's number, and I reached him by phone at ten-thirty. I told him that I didn't know exactly why I needed to see him, but I felt I did. I felt he could help me with the Leadership Forum project. Could he meet with me? I told him I was leaving on a plane for Houston at eight-thirty the next morning. Without hesitation, Harman said he'd meet me at six-thirty in the morning at the airport coffee shop.

Mavis and I both met Willis that next morning, and it was another one of those magical meetings. As we parted, Willis said there was only one thing that he felt I absolutely must do: contact Charles Kiefer and Peter Senge in Cambridge, who would be able to help me put together the curriculum. The next day, when I called Kiefer and Senge, I discovered that they were going to be in Houston the next week presenting a paper on "Metanoic Organizations."

I listened to their presentation with a sense of tremendous excitement and discovery. *Metanoia* comes from a Greek word meaning "a fundamental shift of mind." Simply put, in Senge and Kiefer's terms, these organizations operate with a conviction that they can shape their destiny. The climate created within such an organization can have profound effects on people, particularly by nurturing an understanding of and a responsibility for the larger social systems within which the individual and the organization operate. In a such an organization, individuals aligned around an appropriate vision can have extraordinary influence in the world. Antecedents of this idea can be found in many places: the management theories of Douglas McGregor, the writing of systems theorists like Jay Forrester, and even the basic beliefs in freedom and self-determination expressed in the founding of the United States.

Charlie, Peter, and I met later that afternoon for a couple of hours. I poured my story out to them. At the conclusion, I told them that their concepts were highly aligned with the fundamental themes of the Leadership Forum: that at the heart of effective societal leadership is a deep sense of purposefulness; that there is extraordinary power in a group committed to a common vision; that successful leadership depends upon a fundamental shift of being, including a deep commitment to the dream and a passion for serving versus being driven by the pursuit of status and power; that development of the inner education of the fellows was a basic building block of our entire program and I needed help in that department.

They told me that building organizations around the concept of metanoia was merely another stage in the evolution of the democratic concept. Such organizations represent a striving toward a more natural form of organization that would be more consistent with the true nature of people and the nature of complex social systems. Peter said that two hundred years ago, Tom Paine stirred a nation with the appeal that it was only "common sense" that men should rule themselves. Shortly after that, the Declaration of Independence was written to align the diverse interests of the American colonies, proclaiming "We hold these truths to be self-evident. . . ." Peter and Charlie said that the emerging metanoic organizations they worked with derived their inspiration and orientation from this same vision of democracy as a natural social order. They said that the work that I was all about and what they were all about was the same. And they agreed to help.

That day I had instantly felt a deep connection with and love for both Charlie and Peter. It was a mutual feeling, and still exists among all three of us. Charlie and Peter helped me understand how to teach some of the most important concepts of authentic leadership, but they also did more. They helped to sustain me during the most trying times that I had in building the Leadership Forum, and they helped me to see what I was all about.

><+>·O·<+><

During this early process of gathering the team, I raised the seed money to start the operation. In less than three weeks, I raised $750,000. Tom Fatjo, who had given me the first nudge, stepped forward to fulfill his promise to me. He gave me $250,000. One of his business partners, A. Mannai, gave me another $250,000. The balance came from a Houston charitable foundation.

One of the highlights of this era of the start-up (1981 and 1982) was gathering all of these leaders in thinking, these national treasures, together in one room to brainstorm and create the program. We would open these meetings by declaring, "We've got a clean slate. How would you go about creating a program for these successor generation leaders who have risen almost to the top of whatever they have chosen to do and who have so much innate capacity to give to their community and to their country?"

Most of these people had never been in the same room together, but all of them knew of one another by reputation and by reading the books or articles each had written. John Gardner came to Houston several times, as did Henry Steele Commager, James MacGregor Burns, Harlan Cleveland, Warren Bennis, Rosabeth Moss Kantor, Tom Cronin, Elsa Porter, Admiral James Bond Stockdale, Willis Harman, Don Michael, one of the great thinkers on collaborative leadership, and David Campbell of the Center for Creative Leadership.

In those early years, Warren Bennis, Tom Cronin, and Harlan Cleveland took a major role in the development of the curriculum. Harlan and his committee formulated their views as a series of eight propositions:

1. The trouble with American leaders is their lack of self-knowledge.

2. The trouble with American leaders is their lack of appreciation for the nature of leadership itself.

3. The trouble with American leaders is their focus on concepts that separate (communities, nations, disciplines, fields, methods, etc.), rather than concepts that express our interconnectedness.

4. The trouble with American leaders is their ignorance of the world and of U.S. interdependence—their lack of worldmindedness.

5. The trouble with American leaders is their inattention to values—forgetting to ask "Why?" and "What for?"

6. The trouble with American leaders is that they do not know how to make changes, to analyze "social architecture" [Warren Bennis's term], and to create a team to make something different happen.

7. The trouble with American leaders is an insufficient appreciation of the relevance of stakeholders; of the implications of pluralism; and of the fact that nobody is in charge, and therefore each leader is partly in charge of the situation as a whole.

8. The trouble with American leaders is that they are not
sufficiently aware of the context, or the external environment,
of whatever it is they are responsible for doing.

These ideas acted as the guiding principles of our program.

⤙•⬦•○•⬦•⤚

Often during this process of gathering the team I would sit back and rub my eyes in disbelief. I felt somehow strongly disconnected as if I were a lightning rod causing all these people to gather around—all these energies to come together. At such times I felt more like an observer, watching the story unfold, as if this were happening through me but not by me. There was a lot of synthesizing and merging going on among the trustees, and it was fascinating to watch this develop.

In this process, I began to understand that in some way there was a single larger conversation starting to unfold, and that my role was as the convener in helping to nurture this process along. In those early days, each step along the way was marked by a sense of wonder in me—that all these people were gathering together and that they seemed to operate as with one mind.

I remembered the story David Halberstam tells in *The Amateurs* about the moment of swing in rowing.

> When most oarsmen talked about their perfect moments in a boat, they referred not so much to winning a race, as to the feel of the boat, all eight oars in the water together, the synchronization almost perfect. In moments like these, the boat seemed to lift right out of the water. Oarsmen called that the moment of *swing*.

Olympic contender John Biglow loved that moment, too, but "what he liked most about it, he said, was that it allowed you to *trust* the other men in the boat. A boat did not have swing unless everyone was putting out in exact measure, and because of that, and only because of that, there was the possibility of true trust among oarsmen."

People and groups think of themselves as separate. But if we could learn how to dialogue with one another at a deep level, like the trustees who were convening, we would find ways to relate to one another that would dissolve the perception of separateness. This became our central focus: finding a way to dissolve the perception of separateness among the fellows in order that they might work together and experience one another on a different plane. Once they have experienced the shift to wholeness, they cannot deny the insight that results. Relatively few individuals working together in this way could have a profound effect on society because, according to Bohm, their consciousness is already woven into all consciousness. I began devoting all of my energy to this central idea, and over the ensuing three or four years, began to witness some of the most exciting and powerful moments of group communication and collective action imaginable.

15. THE WILDERNESS EXPERIENCE: A GATEWAY TO DIALOGUE

To venture causes anxiety, but not to venture is to lose one's self. . . . And
to venture in the highest is precisely to be conscious of one's self.

—Søren Kierkegaard

By early 1982 we had raised sufficient capital for the start-up phase; we had our
trustees, advisors, and staff all in place; and we had designed the organizational
structure for the delivery of the program. The plan was to bring together twenty to
twenty-five leaders from each of several communities nationwide, including
corporate executives, public officials, and leaders in education, labor, religion, art,
the media, and the professions. These individuals would constitute a class, which
would be administered and supported by a local chapter. Annual classes out of each
community would convene beginning in June of each year.

Our biggest challenge at this point was to design the specific program segments
within the very tight constraints that were given: it must be a world-class program;
it must meet the objectives set forth in the trustees' guiding principles; it must be
deliverable simultaneously in multiple communities; and it must meet tight
budgetary guidelines. After running a pilot program in Houston that tested many of
the specific program segments under design, I began pursuing one of my earliest and
strongest hunches. From the beginning, I had known that our curriculum must
include a segment to foster an intense engagement that would not only get the
fellows past the blocks Bohm talked about, but that would also alter the way they
experienced one another.

This would be the gateway to the inner education of the fellows, which was at the very heart of the program. Bohm said we had to find a way to communicate with people that would dissolve the blocks within them and transform them. In London, Bohm had talked to me about the human capacity for collective intelligence, for generative conversation and resulting coordinated action:

> At present, people create barriers between each other by their fragmentary thought. Each one operates separately. When these barriers have dissolved, then there arises one mind, where they are all one unit, but each person also retains his or her own individual awareness. That one mind will still exist when they are separate, and when they come together, it will be as if they hadn't separated. . . . It's actually a single intelligence that works with people who are moving in relationship with one another. . . . If you had a number of people who really pulled together and worked together in this way, it would be so remarkable.

Most people had a block, according to Bohm, because "they feel they could never make a difference, and therefore they never face the possibility because it's too disturbing, too frightening. . . . There must be a communication that will take place that will dissolve that block." My hunch in 1982 was that a wilderness experience constructed according to the principles proposed by Kurt Hahn of the Gordenston School in Scotland was the most effective way to dissolve that block.

During the early part of World War II, Kurt Hahn had been commissioned by the Royal Navy to help determine how to deal with an unusual phenomenon. When the Royal Navy's ships would go down in the frigid North Sea, a large proportion of the sailors would die before help could arrive. But a strange thing was happening—those who survived were almost all older people in their forties. The younger, seemingly more fit and hearty people in their twenties, were perishing.

Hahn studied the situation and came to the conclusion that the older people were surviving because they had been through the trials and tribulations and exigencies of life itself. They had grown in body, mind, and spirit, and had the will to live and to deal with extremely demanding new challenges. The younger people simply had not developed that kind of inner capacity. Hahn created a new educational experience that helped these young people develop the kind of staying power that was necessary. They began surviving in the same numbers as the older men. After the war, Hahn brought this concept to America, and the result was the Outward Bound movement.

Hahn's theory was that the limits to our potential are mostly imagined. His courses were designed to present the participants with a series of increasingly difficult tasks. First you accomplish something you never conceived you could have accomplished. The next day you accomplish something even more amazing, and on succeeding days you keep surpassing your previous accomplishments. By the end of the course, your image of what is possible for yourself is altered forever.

Hahn's second objective was to heighten the participants' sense of duty and compassion to those around them. No one can fully explain what propels individuals toward particular acts of compassion and altruism, but it's clear that there are principles in human beings that drive them to help one another. Hahn believed that people are social beings and learn best in a group setting. He formed learning groups which amounted to tight communities that created an environment stressing the value and need to care for others. He believed that these deep, primitive human impulses could best be strengthened in an elemental setting.

In 1982, when I began working on the wilderness experience as part of the curriculum, I called the Colorado Outward Bound School and spoke to Reola Phelps, who was the executive director of their newly formed executive program. I told her a little bit about the Leadership Forum and asked for a meeting. The following week I went to Colorado and met Reola and three of her colleagues, David Chrislip, Eric Malmborg, and Peter O'Neil. It was an effortless and very special gathering, and we all shared a full understanding of how the program would be constructed and delivered. I told them my dreams about the Leadership Forum and shared with them what I thought it could do for the country and for the world. I knew as we spoke together that we were communicating at a level much higher than words alone and I felt an intense personal connection with them.

As we designed the wilderness segment, we set forth five objectives:

1. Strengthen the fellows' power of self-belief, their feeling of self-efficacy, and the belief that they can accomplish what they set forth to do. It was our intent to give them the clear message that they were using only a fraction of their true capacity. We then would give them solid evidence of that fact.

2. Encourage the fellows to rely on their inner resources that are so seldom tapped, to use their intuition and the ability to extemporize and innovate in the face of uncertainty and ambiguity.

3. Build deep trust and respect among the group, and help each fellow get beyond the devaluing prejudices that we all hold. Build true teamwork among the group and have them experience— perhaps for the first time—what deep alignment in a group feels like. Foster an experience of how a group of leaders from many sectors in a community can coalesce around issues of shared concern and move to successful resolution.

4. Put the fellows in situations that will cause them to reach deeply into themselves and be led into what Bohm called "the generating depth of consciousness which is common to the whole of mankind." Evoke their higher nature and have them experience that we are all connected.

5. Learn from the entire experience how to be flexible and adapt quickly to change and new environments.

The American Leadership Forum program curriculum was tested and in place by 1983. Each class experienced a program of approximately twenty days duration over the course of a year, starting with an orientation session to begin the process of connecting the fellows. The orientation was also designed to prepare them for the wilderness experience, which usually took place in early July, when the weather in the Rocky Mountains was appropriate for rock and peak climbing. The program was predominantly experiential, not only in the wilderness segment, but also in other segments, most notably the Leadership in Action segment in which participants learned by doing in the context of a project of value to the community. Annual classes were eventually convened in Houston, Hartford, the state of Oregon, Tacoma, and Silicon Valley.

The wilderness experience was designed as a six-day segment. The fellows usually arrived at the base camp in the late afternoon on a Friday and departed six days later. During this time the group undertook rock climbing, classroom instruction, outdoor exercises of various types, a climb of a fourteen-thousand-foot peak, a twenty-four-hour solo experience (camping in the wilderness alone), and the closing ceremonies. The group work was broken up often with plenty of time for individual reflection and journal writing. Watches and clocks were not used during the entire experience.

The full year's program was ultimately designed to be an inner journey for the fellows, not unlike the hero's journey Joseph Campbell wrote about in *The Hero with a Thousand Faces*. The quest was a transformative cycle consisting roughly of three stages: separation or departure; the trials, failures, and victories, including a supreme ordeal; and finally, the return to and reintegration into society. The wilderness experience was itself a mini hero's journey—an inner journey of discovery and personal renewal. I personally loved the wilderness segment of the program, and for the first several years went through the entire program with one of the classes. Over the years, I witnessed the most moving and profound changes in both individuals and groups, and I was, in the process, personally transformed.

Part of the magic of the experience lay in the sheer beauty of the setting: the breathtaking sight of the high mountains, the sweep of the sky, the panorama of the great valley. The beauty drives you out of the self for a moment—so that for this time, the self is not. It's that indescribable feeling of coming together, time suspended; of being linked to the universe. But there is a far more primordial aspect to this. For tens of thousands of years, human beings and the wilderness could not be separated—"one has been the context for the other." As this occurred to me time and time again, it reminded me of the basic notion in quantum theory about the inseparability of the observer and the observed.

At the very beginning of the six days, the larger group was divided into two subgroups for purposes of conducting various exercises. At the conclusion of each exercise, each subgroup formed a circle and dialogued about the lessons learned. Each day the two groups came together for larger conversations. There was also a constant shifting from group dialogue to inner dialogue, when the participants took time alone to reflect and write in their journals. The setting, the high adventure, and the group endeavor all contributed to a certain state of being, out of which the participants could listen and speak and learn more effectively.

Each person was tested in his or her own way: fear of height, fear of being alone, fear of failure, fear of looking foolish. Early on in the experience, it became clear that one had to rely on the group to make it. An intense personal connection among the group developed—the kind of connection people long for and seldom find as they reach adulthood.

Each exercise was designed to build true trust among the fellows, those perfect moments David Halberstam spoke of, the moments of swing. Climbing the 150-foot rock face was the first such experience and perhaps the most powerful. Here's how one Hartford fellow described it:

> I am sitting at the top of a cliff and I mentally compose this letter, tied to a rope anchored in rock. The early morning sun has given way to a cold drizzle. My hands hold tightly the rope which drops down to a partner who is inching her way up the cliff.
>
> The experience I describe is that of belaying a fellow climber up a cliff. No relation between two people is as intimate and so completely based on trust. The rope is there for protection, not, as some might imagine, to hold onto. My partner is invisible until the last few feet when her head emerges over the edge of a rock six feet below me. What holds us together is a carefully crafted system of verbal calls, and the subtle tension on the rope. Those are signs of a contract between us. No one, least of all an inexperienced novice, would commit life itself to the side of an exposed cliff without complete trust in the belayer.

The fourth and fifth days were spent in preparing for and executing the peak climb. In the early years of the program, we climbed Mt. Elbert, the highest peak in Colorado at 14,300 feet. The climb and return usually took about fourteen hours. It was a physical, mental, and emotional experience, and one that was always special to me.

I'll never forget the first peak climb I did with the Houston Class I. After spending the night at a high base camp, we arose at three in the morning to pack our gear and eat breakfast. We had to reach the summit before noon because of the risk of thunderstorms that often form later in the day at high altitudes. Lightning can be particularly deadly above the treeline, where we would all be so exposed.

We struck out at the appointed time in pitch darkness. We climbed for hours below the treeline, and finding our orientation in these conditions was difficult. We took wrong courses and had to double back a number of times. The grade was extremely steep, and backtracking was a painful affair because we all recognized the noon deadline and the need to conserve energy. Along the way, a hundred kindnesses occurred every hour. Gender and racial differences had long since melted away, and all the way to the summit, people were helping people.

As we passed the treeline at around twelve thousand feet, we saw nothing but rocks. The wind was howling, the temperature was frigid, and at first we could see no vegetation whatsoever. But after a time, we began to notice the absolutely magnificent, tiny, tiny flowers that grow in the summertime upon the top of the mountain. We had to look hard to see them because they were in between the rocks where just the barest hint of sunlight falls on the tiny patches of soil. The colors were intense—deep, deep yellows and purples, and the most crimson of all crimsons. There they were, not only surviving, but flourishing. As we observed them, we drew strength from the little flowers that could thrive in this kind of environment. We called it the "land of the one-inch giants."

But there was more to it than that; I found myself treasuring these little flowers but knowing that I wouldn't pick one for anything in the world. It was a deeply moving aesthetic experience that did not move me to possess the object; the beauty was in the simple beholding of it. I could see the rhythm of the universe up there—the relationship of the sunlight to the little flower, and of the soil to the flower, and of the mist to the flower and to the soil, and of the sunlight that broke through the cloud and the mist and the fog. As I slowly moved through the land of the one-inch giants, I felt, once again, completely in accord with the universe.

The pain of the last fifteen hundred feet was intense for all of us. There is very little oxygen at this height, and our lungs were burning. Every muscle in my body was aching, and I wondered if I could take another step. Many of us experienced altitude sickness, dizziness, and sheer exhaustion. Muscle cramps, severely blistered feet—the group fought through it all. The wind was high, and the windchill factor was thirty degrees below zero. But when we broke through the last ridge to the summit, it was an indescribably sublime experience: the whole horizon opened up, and with this my consciousness expanded as well.

We were all overcome with emotion. We formed a circle and held hands in silence for a long time, the vast panorama lying behind us. It was as if we were literally on top of the world. There were no boundaries between any of us, and time seemed to stand still. We were communicating at a deep level with one another—

much like my experience with the ermine. Finally, Don Wukasch, a Houston heart surgeon, spoke, reciting by memory from René Daumal:

> You cannot stay on the summit forever; you have to come down. . . . So why bother in the first place? Just this: What is above knows what is below, but what is below does not know what is above. In climbing, take careful note of the difficulties along your way; for as you go up, you can observe them. Coming down, you will no longer see them, but you will know they are there if you have observed them well.
>
> There is an art of finding one's direction in the lower regions by the memory of what one saw higher up. When one can no longer see, one can at least still know.

Again we stood in silence, absorbed in the moment. Then Rabbi Roy Walter spoke in Hebrew:

> Blessed are you O Lord our God, Ruler of the universe, who has given us life, sustained us in life, and brought us together to share this moment in time.

>--+◇·O·◇+--<

The return to the high base camp was made as quickly as possible to avoid the thunderstorms. When we reached the base camp, it was almost dark, and everyone was exhausted. We changed out of our wet clothes—we had encountered rain on the way down. Dry socks were heaven. We ate a light meal and broke camp for the solo experience, each person camping alone in the wilderness with only a few necessities and a solo tarp. It was an opportunity to reflect upon the lessons of experience, to integrate as best we could what had occurred over the past week, and to write in our journals.

Being out there alone in the wilderness for me was at once a powerful and peaceful experience. It was like visiting the great cathedral at Chartres. I could feel the energy field, and it was as if I were participating in divinity itself. I was in awe of the sheer wonder and beauty of it all. Over the hours that passed, the recognition that I was in the presence of something larger than the human dimension grew greater and greater.

The following day, after breaking solo camp, the group came together at the high base camp for a dialogue around the campfire. We sat in a circle around the fire. The circle is a powerful symbol suggesting no beginning, no end. It speaks to us of the journey itself. We had been on a journey for a week, and now we were contemplating a larger journey. Within the bounded circle the power of the community among us continued. The same feeling was present as had been with us at the summit—the silence, the speaking only from the heart, the harmony of being, the awe and reverence for the beauty around us. The principal difference, though, was that we spent several hours in this dialogue, and matters of substance were brought up and dealt with—matters which, under normal circumstances, are undiscussable: prejudice, race, gender issues. The diversity of the group added great power to the dialogue. There was a lot of emotion, but also deep listening and learning. At this stage the fellows were operating as "open systems." They had entered the experience with sets of assumptions about themselves— images of who they were, and what they could and could not do. One by one, as the fellows accomplished so much more than they conceived was possible, these images were destroyed.

In addition, the fellows had participated in classroom work based upon the Leadership and Mastery course devised by Kiefer and Senge. That had been a powerful experience in and of itself, resulting in a suspension of prior assumptions about human nature, consciousness, and the fundamental nature of things.

On the final day, just a few hours before the group boarded the bus to Denver for the flight home, the closing ceremony took place. This was a final collective conversation at which each person presented his or her totem: an object found during the solo experience that best symbolized his or her feelings about the wilderness experience and its meaning.

><+>·O·<+><

By almost any measure, we felt the design of the wilderness experience had accomplished what we had wanted: to provide the gateway to those fundamental shifts of mind and being, so necessary to servant leadership. The theme consistently expressed through the totem ceremony was "the peace and love we have shared together," the "deep connection" felt among people who care so much, the "almost transcendental identification I feel with the other humans here," the power of the physical environment which "borders on the mystical," and the "metamorphosis occurring within." I marveled at the consistency of these statements, regardless of the background of the person speaking: a city mayor, a chief of police, a labor leader, a CEO, a leader from the inner city, a journalist, you name it—these themes cut across every category, gender, race, and ethnic line in the community.

Over the years we heard the fellows express these same themes again and again as they presented their totems at the closing ceremonies. We had found a way to remove the blocks Bohm had talked to me about, but I began to wonder whether there was a way to accomplish this with a less elaborate and expensive process. As it turned out, David Bohm and his colleagues were in the process of providing at least a partial answer.

16. DIALOGUE: THE POWER OF COLLECTIVE THINKING

> From time to time, (the) tribe (gathered) in a circle.
> They just talked and talked and talked, apparently to no purpose.
> They made no decisions. There was no leader. And everybody could
> participate. There may have been wise men or wise women who were
> listened to a bit more—the older ones—but everybody could talk.
> The meeting went on, until it finally seemed to stop for no reason at all and
> the group dispersed. Yet after that, everybody seemed to know what to do,
> because they understood each other so well. Then they could get together
> in smaller groups and do something or decide things.
>
> —David Bohm, *On Dialogue*

Bohm had shared with me in London an explicit mental model of the way he believed the world works and the way he believed human beings learn and think. To Bohm it was clear that humans have an innate capacity for collective intelligence. They can learn and think together, and this collaborative thought can lead to coordinated action. We are all connected and operate within living fields of thought and perception. The world is not fixed but is in constant flux; accordingly, the future is not fixed, and so can be shaped. Humans possess significant tacit knowledge—we know more than we can say. The question to be resolved: how to remove the blocks and tap into that knowledge in order to create the kind of future we all want?

By 1983, Bohm was devoting much of his time to exploring this issue of collective thinking and communication. Over the next ten years a significant amount of progress would be made toward understanding this entire process, which Bohm simply called "dialogue."

In May 1984, what was intended as a weekend seminar consisting of lectures and discussions developed into what Bohm called "the awakening of the process of dialogue itself as a free flow of meaning among all the participants." That weekend marked a sort of watershed in Bohm's work on this subject and is documented in the book *Unfolding Meaning*.

Although development of a theory of dialogue was far from complete, by 1994, in part because of the work of the Dialogue Project at the MIT Center for Organizational Learning led by William N. Isaacs, dialogue began to be seen as a breakthrough of major significance in a number of emergent fields of human activity: in organizational learning, in the process of collective inquiry, and, significantly, in the way humans might govern themselves.

As mentioned previously, the word "dialogue," as used by Bohm, comes from two Greek roots, *dia* and *logos*, suggesting "meaning flowing through." This stands in stark contrast to the word "debate," which means "to beat down," or even "discussion," which has the same root as "percussion" and "concussion"—"to break things up."

Bohm pointed out that a great deal of what we call discussion is not deeply serious in the sense that there are all sorts of things which are nonnegotiable—the "undiscussables." No one mentions the undiscussables—they're just there, lying beneath the surface, blocking deep, honest, heart-to-heart communication. Furthermore, we all bring basic assumptions with us, our own mental maps, about the meaning of life, how the world operates, our own self-interest, our country's interest, our religious interest, and so forth. Our basic assumptions are developed from our early days, our teachers, our family, what we read. We hold these assumptions so deeply that we become identified with them, and when these assumptions are challenged, we defend them with great emotion. Quite often, we do this unconsciously.

Bohm likened these basic assumptions and deeply held convictions to computer programs in people's minds. These programs take over against the best of intentions, and they produce their own intentions. This fragmentation of thought is reinforced by a world view inherited from the sixteenth century, which saw the cosmos as a great machine. Thus, "ordinary thought in society is incoherent—it's going in all sorts of directions canceling each other out."

But if people were to think together in a coherent way, it would have tremendous power. If there was an opportunity for sustained dialogue over a period of time, we would have coherent movement of thought, not only at the conscious level we all recognize, but even more importantly at the tacit level, the unspoken level which cannot be described. Dialogue does not require people to agree with each other. Instead, it encourages people to participate in a pool of shared meaning that leads to aligned action. As Isaacs and his research group at MIT confirmed, out of this new shared meaning, people can and will take coordinated and effective action without necessarily agreeing about the reasons for the action.

Bohm compared dialogue to superconductivity. "In superconductivity, electrons cooled to a very low temperature act more like a coherent whole than as separate parts. They flow around obstacles without colliding with one another, creating no resistance and very high energy. At higher temperatures, however, they begin to act like separate parts, scattering into a random movement and losing momentum." In dialogue, the goal is to create a special environment in which a different kind of relationship among parts can come into play—one that reveals both high energy and high intelligence.

As I look back on the research and development Bohm did on dialogue during the last years of his life, it's been interesting for me to note how the principles he formulated were consistently playing out during the course of the Forum program: at the fellows' orientation, where they gathered initially to become acquainted; through the wilderness experience; at the midcourse retreat; during the hard work of the class project; and at the closing ceremonies as well as the postgraduation class retreats. The shared experience and deep trust developed in the wilderness experience allowed the fellows to enter into dialogue in a variety of circumstances, in small groups as well as much larger ones. After a couple of years of these experiences, I could sense the "field" forming as we entered into true dialogue. This distinct and special feeling would fill the space around us, and at these times I knew we were communicating on a different plane. It was unmistakable. Most often during these times I would say or contribute very little; I would be deeply involved in the communication, listening and absorbing what was happening. Each time these were powerful, moving, and extremely special experiences for me and for the others involved.

At times, dialogue was used to resolve complex issues facing the group, such as those revolving around their class projects. Invariably the conversations would be tedious and frustrating, particularly to the kinds of action-oriented, get-it-done-today individuals making up the classes. But often this process would lead to coordinated action that resulted in highly important contributions to the community involved. In other instances, the dialogue would not have a strategic focus, but would yield important results at a later date. Out of the collective listening, important new insights were gleaned. The fellows reported to me time and time again deep personal change flowing from the ongoing dialogue that was sustained over the course of the year.

When a particular dialogue was "completed," it was not over. Dialogue was not a single circumstance in the program, but turned out to be a way of life with the fellows—a way of life to which they became committed. It had a transformational effect upon many of the people. Repeatedly, fellows would refer to the "mysterious power of the collective" they would experience.

It's a funny thing about dialogue: there's a wave/particle–like aspect to it. When it's present, you know it. You can't fake dialogue. Yet when you focus on it too hard, and try to capture the process, you change it, and it collapses and vanishes.

><+>-o-<+><

There were times that dialogue was used in another special way—to communicate the power of the ALF experience to potential major funders. We would convene a group of the fellows to tell how ALF had touched their lives and the lives of their communities. I stumbled onto this process one evening in Houston when I invited one of the key officers of the Ford Foundation and his deputy to a dinner and meeting with a dozen or so fellows. What ensued after dinner was an uninterrupted three-hour dialogue among the fellows. The people from the Ford Foundation found it to be one of the most moving experiences they'd ever had.

One of the most important times this occurred was in 1988 when we were seeking funding from the Luce Foundation in New York. We had a number of meetings with the Foundation executives at Luce, which resulted in a site visit to Hartford by Henry Luce, Jr. We invited a dozen fellows to attend lunch and dialogue with Mr. Luce and his colleagues.

John Filer, Chairman of the Aetna Insurance Company, opened the conversation with a beautiful set of remarks, calling the group assembled "a magnificent coalition of the unalike." I then suggested that the fellows might want to share with Mr. Luce and the other officials of the Luce Foundation what they could about the Leadership Forum, what it meant to them personally, and what had occurred in the community as a result of the establishment of the chapter. We had not rehearsed or planned ahead for any of this. A long silence ensued and eventually one of the fellows spoke up.

Eddie Perez described a Leadership Forum project in Stow Village, a public housing development with over a thousand people, mostly Latinos and African-Americans, living in abject poverty. People there felt hopeless and defeated. Most of the residents were single mothers with several children. The project objective was to take fifty families and construct a program through which these people could attain economic independence through substantial employment. It seemed like a massive undertaking, but this class of fellows wanted to test the momentum, the excitement, and the vitality that had been brought to bear within that group.

Eddie told how the program had begun and how it was progressing on many fronts. He said that it was being hailed as a model that could be replicated throughout the country. Indeed, a separate group was attempting to replicate the program in two other public housing projects in Hartford. Eddie said that one of the keys to the success was the strong linkage between the business community and the public sector. There were several brick walls presented that needed to be torn down, and it was the people with position and power in big business that could make it happen most quickly. He cited the following example: The project had progressed substantially. A number of the women had gone through the job skills program, transportation and child care had been arranged, the women had learned how to dress appropriately for an office environment, and job positions had been secured—not just dead-end jobs, but jobs with a real future for advancement and personal satisfaction. Everything was set to go, and then the brick wall was hit. The new employers' insurance would cover the worker, but for the first year, the medical insurance would not cover the entire family. It would be too cost-prohibitive, and the policy would not allow it.

These women simply could not afford to go to work and leave their children without medical benefits. The welfare program provided this, but, at least in the initial stage of work, the employers could not. Eddie worked and worked and could find no way around it. Finally, in desperation he picked up the phone and called Jim

Grigsby, a fellow from his ALF class. Jim headed a billion-dollar division of CIGNA, one of the largest insurance companies in the world. When Eddie called, Jim's secretary took the message and politely told Eddie that Jim had been out of town for quite some time, and it would be a very long time before he could get back to him. It was the kind of polite brush-off that secretaries are taught to give.

That afternoon, Jim came to his office and was met with a huge stack of pink telephone slips. He flipped through them and toward the bottom he saw Eddie's call slip. It said, "Eddie Perez, ALF, needs help. Please call." That same day, Jim returned Eddie's call, and the conversation went something like this: "Eddie, Jim here. I'm returning your call. What can I do for you?"

"I need to come see you. We've got a crisis of major proportions on the Stow Village Project, and I really need your help."

"Well, why don't you just tell me over the telephone, and we will see what we can do."

Eddie told Jim the story, and Jim said, "Eddie, I've got it. I've got the picture. Give me a week or ten days to see what my people can do, and I'll be back to you."

Within a week, Jim called Eddie back and said, "Eddie, I've got the problem solved. Here is what we'll do." And he proceeded to tell him how he found a way for the business to be underwritten. Eddie looked at Mr. Luce and the others, and he said, "Listen, a year ago, if I had placed a call like that to Jim Grigsby at CIGNA, I wouldn't have gotten past his secretary. There's no way he would have returned my call, and there's no way we could have solved that problem. I'm telling you that we are all members of one community here, and we are all out to help Hartford. The right people are connected now. We in the neighborhood community know how things operate, and we know how to get things done, but we can't get them done without the cooperation of people in the power structure. We need their help, and we need it sometimes very quickly. The American Leadership Forum makes that possible."

And that's the way it went around the table. The fellows, each in their own way, told of the transformation that was taking place in the Hartford community. Each told a personal story and each built on the other's story. When there was a brief silence, another fellow would interject a word, a few sentences, or a story to underscore the point being made. No one talked over the other. Later the fellows observed that they were listening to others saying their own thoughts. The flow of conversation built and built. Each statement, each point, each story dovetailed and reinforced another. It was like the weaving of an intricate, beautiful tapestry—as if they were speaking by design—but of course there was no prior rehearsal. The flow of meaning was incredible. The group was working as a whole, and there was common participation in thinking, as if it were one thought being formed together. And you could feel the whole room fall into this symphony of conversation. As I witnessed this unfold, I thought back to the way Bill Russell described those moments when he was playing for the Celtics.

John Zacharian, the editor of the editorial page of *The Hartford Courant*, told about his successful campaign to add the first African-American member to the advisory editorial board of his paper. Hernan LaFontaine, the Superintendent of Schools, told of the jobs program that he and fellows from his class had instituted to provide placement for two hundred unemployed youths who were graduating from the Hartford high schools. The program was taken over by a unit of the Chamber of Commerce and continued to be highly successful. This was only made possible by the joint cooperation among school leaders and neighborhood leaders and top business leaders, who could insure that the right kind of job opportunities were made available.

Bernie Sullivan, the Chief of Police, and Merilee Milstead, a local labor leader, told of how they had first met when Chief Sullivan had incarcerated her during the course of a strike in Hartford. For years, there had been violence and bloodshed during these strikes. The next time Milstead and Chief Sullivan met, they were fellows in the Forum Class I. By the end of that year, they had agreed to do things differently. When the next strike occurred, Milstead called Chief Sullivan and said, "We are getting ready to strike. Let's do it the way that we agreed." Chief Sullivan went to his men and said, "There's going to be a strike led by Merilee Milstead. I want us to go out there and keep order, but leave your riot gear at home." They went out. There was an entirely peaceful strike. No bloodshed and not one incarceration. An absolute first in many years. Around the table the stories went, one after another, just like that.

At the end there was a long but comfortable silence. Then Henry Luce stood up and said, "I knew I would be impressed with this program because of what I'd read about it. But I was not prepared for what I encountered here. You will receive our support." Within two months we received a $450,000 grant from the Luce Foundation, the largest public affairs grant that the Luce Foundation had ever given.

———————

What occurred in Hartford that day with Henry Luce and his colleagues was an exercise in collective leadership. These men and women sitting in dialogue together were exercising a collective form of leadership that simply cannot be provided by a single individual. Over the years I've thought more and more about this notion of highly effective leadership. I've come to believe that this is at the heart of what is needed in the world today. When people sit in dialogue together, they are exercising leadership as a whole. This is nothing less than the unfolding of the generative process. It's the way that thought participates in creating, but it can only be done collectively.

This is not something I fully understood during the days I worked with ALF, even though I witnessed this powerful phenomenon time and time again. The way we generally thought about it as we were designing the program was that parts are primary. In a coalition-building model, our tacit assumption is that we're separate individuals, and we have to build a coalition. We usually do that through various kinds of trade-offs and deals—hopefully "win-win" kinds of arrangements that we can all live with.

But in dialogue, you operate with a very different premise, actually, a completely different frame of reference. In dialogue, you're not building anything, you're allowing the whole that exists to become manifest. It's a deep shift in consciousness away from the notion that parts are primary.

People always say "We have to step back and see the big picture here," as if we have to go from seeing the parts to constructing a whole. But the whole already exists; it's just that we're locked into a frame of reference that keeps us from perceiving it. In dialogue, the whole shows up and is manifested by individuals later as they take action.

"Seeing things whole" amounts to an inner shift in awareness and consciousness. Martin Buber captured this notion beautifully as he was reflecting on what this means between people:

> Just as the melody is not made up of notes nor the verse of words nor the statue of lines, but they must be tugged and dragged till their unity has been scattered into these many pieces, so with the man to whom I say *Thou*. I can take out from him the colour of his hair, or of his speech, or of his goodness. I must continually do this. But each time I do it he ceases to be *Thou*.

17. LESSONS: ENCOUNTERING
THE TRAPS

Where you stumble, there your treasure lies.

—Joseph Campbell

One day in 1987 I was with a class of Forum fellows in Portland, Oregon, telling them about the journey I had taken in the creation of the Forum—the good times, and the trials and tribulations as well. Afterwards the executive director of the Oregon chapter, Mary Ann Buchannan, came up and said, "Joe, what you just told us seemed like it was straight out of Joseph Campbell's *The Hero with a Thousand Faces.*" I told her I didn't know who Joseph Campbell was and had never read any of his books. She was very surprised because his most recent book, *The Power of Myth,* had been widely read. She explained that Campbell, who had recently died, was an authority on mythology and a preeminent scholar. She sent me his books, and I was absolutely struck by what I read. In *The Hero with a Thousand Faces* Campbell presents a composite picture of the heroic quest, which is an archetype of the change process humans and organizations alike can go through. Not only did this picture look startlingly like the journey I had taken through the past fifteen years, but it tracked precisely the fundamental ideas expressed by Robert Greenleaf in *Servant Leadership*: The ultimate aim of the servant leader's quest is to find the resources of character to meet his or her destiny—to find the wisdom and power to serve others.

Upon reading this, a great peacefulness came over me. For the first time since I started down this path, I felt affirmed and understood. I had felt so alone throughout this whole affair, I had actually felt half-crazy sometimes. It was only upon reading Campbell that I started integrating what had happened within myself and really understanding some of it.

Campbell's picture begins with the "wasteland," the inauthentic life. Old concepts, ideals, and emotional patterns no longer fit; a time for passing the threshold is at hand. The call to adventure comes in many ways both subtle and explicit over the years. It is the call to service, giving our life over to something larger than ourselves, the call to become what we were meant to become—the call to achieve our "vital design."

Some who are called to the adventure choose to go. Others may wrestle for years with fearfulness and denial before they are able to transcend that fear. We tend to deny our destiny because of our insecurity, our dread of ostracism, our anxiety, and our lack of courage to risk what we have. Down deep we know that to cooperate with fate brings great personal power and responsibility. If we engage our destiny, we are yielding to the design of the universe, which is speaking through the design of our own person. In the face of refusal, we continue our restlessness, and then, as if from nowhere, comes the guide: something or someone to help us toward the threshold of adventure. This may take the form of voices within or people who guide us to see the way.

When we say yes to the call, we cross the threshold of adventure. At this moment of decision, Buber says "And even this is not what we 'ought to' do: rather . . . we cannot do otherwise." This is the point where our freedom and destiny merge. "Here I stand. I can do no other," said Martin Luther.

We pass through the gates of the known into the void, a domain without maps. The perilous journey begins, and we encounter a series of tests, trials, and ordeals. It is a place of both terror and opportunity.

If we have truly committed to follow our dream, there exists beyond ourselves and our conscious will a powerful force that helps us along the way and nurtures our growth and transformation. Our journey is guided by invisible hands with infinitely greater accuracy than is possible through our unaided conscious will. Campbell says it is the "supernatural assisting force" that attends "the elect through the whole course of his ordeal."

On the journey, inevitably, we will meet with one or more supreme ordeals. These are the tests of our commitment to the direction we have taken, and they provide opportunities to learn from failure. In the later stages of our journey, we cross threshold after threshold, enduring the agony of spiritual growth and breaking through personal limitations. We emerge from the supreme encounter no longer the same person; we "have something more that has grown" in us, says Buber.

Finally, the quest accomplished, we return with the elixir for the restoration of society. It is difficult to leave the bliss of the final stages of the journey, a state of high adventure, to return to the long forgotten place from which we first came, where people who are fractions of themselves imagine themselves to be complete. Upon returning, it is hard to take the return blow of reasonable queries, hard resentment, and good people at a loss to comprehend. And we are returning only to prepare to journey forth once more. But we have returned as a potent new being, prepared to go forth again in service of the community.

Of course, no two adventures are ever the same, and no one can ever seek to replicate another's journey. Nevertheless, the overall cyclic pattern and the stages Campbell presents were startling to me. I found them of absorbing interest, not only for me personally, but for the Leadership Forum itself. This writing expressed the shift I went through and it was very much alive in me. I shared all of this with my colleagues, and eventually we used this material as a metaphor for the odyssey the fellows were taking in ALF.

It's great fun to think of the early part of my journey: the call to adventure that came as an inward tug from the experience of Watergate, when the Colonel and I spent time at the ranch; the pain of my divorce; the reading of many books while on my trip to Europe; the illumination in the Tetons; the gentle nudge that Tom Fatjo gave me with the admonition that I must give my dream my complete attention. I refused the call then and went to London, where eventually my Guide appeared in the experiences in Cairo, those surrounding the death of my nephew, and subsequently in my meeting with David Bohm. Thinking about what occurred just after crossing the threshold—the unseen helping hands—is immensely important to me, and I love to tell that part of the story also.

But as it turns out, in the long run, the most useful part of the journey lay in the lessons I learned during the down times—the inevitable ordeals encountered along the way. Campbell called this the "Road of Trials." "In the vocabulary of the mystics," he said "this is the Second Stage of the Way, that of the 'purification of the self,' when the senses are 'cleaned and humbled'. . . ." In this process we see "not only the whole picture of our present case, but also the clue to what we must do to be saved."

I fell into three traps and in the process almost cost the Forum its very existence. I came face to face with my own shortcomings, and it was only by the grace of God and the dedication and hard work of all my partners that the whole enterprise ultimately survived.

I'm using the term *traps* to refer to anything that causes a regression to old ways of thinking and acting, and thus hinders our becoming a part of the unfolding generative process. The traps are very powerful; paradoxically, at a deep level there is very little substance to them. But when we fall into one of those traps, the consequences are immediate and very unpleasant. It's a devastating experience to be in the state of high flow and to lose it. All the creativity shuts down; all the synchronicity suddenly disappears.

We fall into traps principally when the stakes are really high—when the energy is high, lots is happening, things are going beautifully, and a lot of money is involved. That's when these powerful illusions or habits of thought tend to come into play. When we fall into a trap, a vicious circle can begin to operate, and our situation can go from bad to worse very quickly. But if we are aware of traps and remain alert to their danger, we can largely avoid their consequences.

The traps I fell into were particularly my own, and grew out of my own old habits of thought. Similarly, others on the journey to follow their dreams will confront traps particular to their own old ways of being. I offer the following only as examples of the traps we might confront deep into our journeys, when we are in the highest state of flow and when we feel most connected to the unfolding generative order. As you will see, these traps are closely interconnected—one often grows out of another.

THE TRAP OF RESPONSIBILITY

The trap of responsibility was the most vicious trap for me. I encountered it early in the game, and it plagued me for a number of years. In the early stages of founding the Forum, things were falling into place as if by magic: we put together a world-class board of trustees; we designed a curriculum that met with enormous initial success and acceptance in the pilot run; we raised a significant amount of seed money; and our headquarters and chapter staffs grew rapidly. After the initial success, I began thinking in the deeper recesses of my mind: "Hey, this isn't a dream anymore, it's reality. I've got all these people depending on me. They've bought into the dream. Trustees and founders and fellows have stuck their necks out. There's all this media interest. It's too much—the enormity of it. It's too much."

I began to feel I was indispensable to the whole process, that I was responsible for all the people involved, and that everyone was depending on *me*. The focus was on me instead of on the larger calling.

In this state, the fear factor began multiplying. I reverted to the "old" Joe— clamping down, working twelve-, fifteen-, and eighteen-hour days all week, and eventually on weekends as well. I would wake up in the middle of the night dripping with sweat, thinking of all the people whose jobs depended on me, and worrying about where the necessary operating capital would come from. I felt overwhelmed, overworked, and overstressed, and eventually, my obsessive worry led to panic and anxiety attacks. This is a trap I had often encountered as a trial lawyer, particularly in the earlier days as we were building our practice and I was struggling to make my own mark, apart from being Colonel Jaworski's son.

During these days at ALF, the load seemed unbearable. The longer I stayed in this trap, the worse my situation seemed to get. My productivity and effectiveness went down the drain. I began to experience feelings of inadequacy and loss of confidence. Instead of that effortless feeling, we seemed now to be scrambling all the time, putting out fires. Everything seemed to be more difficult. In this whole process, we failed to use our trustees, our founders, our fellows, and our staff effectively. My passion seemed to be locked up. The spirit that had been so much a part of me in those early days couldn't get through. I wasn't open to the possibility any longer, no longer open to risk and creativity.

Other people might tend to fall into different kinds of traps, but for me, responsibility was the big one. I had to learn to distinguish between *concern* and obsessive *worry*. I could be *concerned* about my partners and colleagues without *worrying* about their well being.

I began to get out of this trap by seeing things the way they really are: I am operating in the flow of the universe. There's nothing special about me that allows me to do this; it's a way of operating that is available for everyone. When you are on this path, a natural sorting process is at work. The people who join you are, in their own way, moving along this same path. You have your love and concern for those operating in this sphere with you, but you don't feel *responsible* for them.

It's all in the way we think about it because the cause of the obsessive worry is a powerful illusion that melts in the face of reality. This trap is really a habit of thought. Once we recognize it as such, it tends to lose its power, and we don't really have to fight it. That's the very nature of these traps: they are habits of thought, and once we recognize them, they tend to disappear. This is not to imply you shouldn't think through the consequences of the worst-case scenarios. But scenario planning is a far cry from obsessive worry, which can sap energy and kill the spirit.

THE TRAP OF DEPENDENCY

The trap of dependency is the flip side of feeling responsible for those on the team. In this trap we feel so dependent upon key staff, or key funders, or key trustee support that we feel the enterprise will fail without that element. This fear leads us to compromise the stand we take for the dream. We don't call things as they really are. We're not really straightforward with people for fear that we will offend them, and they will leave the team. We pussyfoot around instead of speaking from our center. We forget that these key people enrolled in our project in response to the flow and that call from our center. That's why they were attracted in the first place. But in the midst of the trap, we fail to recognize that.

It's not that we don't need others around us. Nothing of real substance will occur unless communities of people start to form around the different kind of commitment we evidence. Rather, it's that we become stuck in believing we need some person *in particular* for the enterprise to succeed.

This trap of dependency stems from our feelings of inadequacy and unworthiness. For me, this trap operated below the surface all across the board. I felt a real dependency on certain key staff, on a number of key trustees, and upon several key funders, and this dependency came close to sinking our enterprise.

The most dangerous point occurred around 1983. When I started the Forum, I had been introduced to Jack Warren, one of the most successful oilmen in Texas in the late 1970s and early 1980s. Jack was a deep believer in the ALF dream and had dedicated himself to helping out in any way possible. He introduced me to his friends, he gave me moral support, and in late 1982, after our pilot program was so successful, he pledged an extremely large gift to be paid in one lump sum. I felt Jack was an absolute treasure, and he became a board trustee. I deeply valued his business judgment, his spirit, and his innate sense of servant leadership. His pledge became a focal point in our action plan. It gave us the staying power to develop the curriculum and test it in one or two regions. With positive results in those chapters, we could then tap into the national foundations. That became the overall strategic plan, which we began executing.

When the oil crisis hit Houston, it crept up on us. In the early stages, everyone thought things would straighten out soon. Jack came to me and said he would have to delay his pledge, but as soon as things turned around, he would meet it. Instead of being flexible and immediately looking for new funding avenues, I remained fixated on the original plan, which revolved around Jack's pledge. Ultimately, the oil crisis deepened. Houston and the state of Texas went into a deep recession, which finally resulted in the collapse of the real estate market, which in turn led to the collapse of most major Texas financial institutions.

As each week and month passed, I remained dependent on the original plan. We had planned to use Jack's gift as an example to other prominent members of the community, so we kept delaying changing the plan, hoping that the crisis would pass.

As I look back on it, I realize that not only was I overly dependent on Jack and a few other key trustees, I also became dependent on our original strategic plan. I *had* to stick to the plan. To change direction was almost a sign of weakness to me; I would tough it out. I relied on the traditional kind of commitment—to stick with something I've started—and it got us into real trouble. I became obsessively anxious about being behind on "the plan."

I was focusing on the process instead of on the result we were trying to create. One of the cornerstones of the Leadership and Mastery course we had included in the wilderness experience is this understanding of the creative orientation. It's critical that you focus on the result and not get attached to any particular process for achieving the result. When we are in the process of creating something, we must have the flexibility of mind to move with what needs to be done. What allows this to happen is precisely the fact that we're not attached to *how* things should be done. It's a little bit like sailing. If you're focused on your course rather than your destination, you're in big trouble. If you were to be blown off course, you would never simply return to the course you were on. No one would sail that way. Rather, you would focus on the destination and set a new course. But that's the way we live our lives. We get attached to our assumptions about how things should get done, and we lose sight of what we're trying to create. This notion of focusing on the results is a fundamental premise of the Leadership and Mastery course.

There are actually two aspects to this cornerstone idea. The first part is the distinction between focusing on the intrinsic result we care about versus focusing on our assumptions about how we need to get there. And the second is the orientation toward the result itself. Most people think of achieving a result in order to get something for ourselves. If we have a dream or a vision we are committed to, and if we look deeply into why we want this vision, we may answer: "Well, if I have that vision, I'll be happy." Or "If I build this enterprise, I will be well respected. . . . I will have made it as a manager. . . . We will make a lot of money." These are the ordinary responses to why we have a dream we want to fulfill. It's actually very rare that people focus on what they want to create *for its own sake*. That's the deeper territory around this principle of focusing on the result. Are we deeply committed to creating what we truly want *for its own sake*? Robert Frost once said "All great things are done for their own sake." When we see our visions and our dreams in this way, it's a subtle but most profound shift. And it's under these circumstances that the "hidden hands" phenomenon begins to occur, and doors open for us that are beyond our imagination.

So at this stage of building ALF, I had reverted to focusing rigidly on the business plan we had devised, instead of focusing on the result, the vision we had intended. This was the exact opposite of what I had done during our most successful earlier phase. At that earlier time, I kept focusing on the dream and had remained highly flexible, going with the flow of things, taking one day at a time, and listening for guidance about the next step. But in this crisis, I clamped down and let my traditional way of operating take over.

In this process, a lot of fear was generated. The further we fell behind in the original game plan, the more fearful I got. Being stuck in the process, the fear of no alternative loomed larger and larger. And a subtle shift took place in me. I began having concerns about how this would reflect on *me*. I began worrying about my reputation and the personal implications if the enterprise failed; I would be embarrassed. This again was exactly 180° opposite from my original way of going.

Before, I had had no fear of failure, and had cared deeply about the dream for its own sake. I was willing to risk everything—my reputation, my position, and even my relationships. I was serving the dream itself because I felt deep down that this was what was intended to happen. I was so intent on the vision that I operated with complete spontaneity and freedom. That's when the doors opened and the upward spiral occurred.

Eventually, I came to realize what I was doing to myself and how I was affecting the whole enterprise. I spent some time with Peter Senge, Charlie Kiefer, and their partner Bob Fritz up in Boston. They helped me to get a grip on the subtle shift that had occurred in my orientation. I did a lot of reflecting and began to get back in touch with that earlier way of operating. Over time I made the necessary adjustment, and we began to focus on the result we intended—a national program to develop servant leadership. We accelerated our original game plan and went after national funding sources: the Hewlett Foundation, the Luce Foundation, the MacArthur Foundation, the Ford Foundation, and others. We were ultimately successful at these following a significant time delay necessary to crank up a national funding drive.

My habit of thought—dependency on the original action plan calling for Texas funding for the first three years of operations—had almost sent us under. That habit of thought was reinforced by my sense that we were not worthy of national funding unless we had established chapters in other regions.

When we began to focus once more on the real result we intended, my old habit of thought lost much of its energy. This was a major learning experience for me. The traps of responsibility and dependency generate a lot of their energy from the fear of no alternative. But there are always alternatives. It's just that we often are unable to see them. Once we realize there is an alternative path, a lot of fear disappears. We start to look at the traps a little more objectively. "There I am again, thinking I'm indispensable. . . . There I am again, overly dependent on a particular person or persons in the organization or on the business plan." It is amazing to me how simple this solution is in the face of such powerful illusions.

One of the most important lessons I learned about the traps was how simple it can be to regain balance when we've lost the flow. Consider the act of walking—a wonderful and powerful metaphor for thinking about this issue. When we're walking or running, we're always in the process of literally falling down. When we move our body forward, we are actually "falling." But we have learned to move quickly and deftly, and so we are "falling" into our next step. If we don't move instantly and with great dexterity, we will fall on our face. As children, we learned our lesson well about the phenomenon of walking and running so that when we're off balance, we can almost effortlessly correct ourselves, regain our balance, and continue on our way.

In ordinary life it's the same way. We lose our balance, as I did for months on end, because we don't understand enough—we don't see we have simple ways to regain it. Most of the martial arts like Akido are oriented around this principle. Simple physical acts like deep breathing can quickly help reestablish our center, our balance, so we can listen to our inner voice once again. It's then that we can see our way more clearly and find our natural path, our natural way of going again.

THE TRAP OF OVERACTIVITY

The third major trap I encountered was one I call overactivity. This trap can manifest most painfully in having people in the organization who are not aligned with the dream, resulting in deep incoherence in the organization.

In the early stages of establishing the Leadership Forum—gathering the team, designing the curriculum, and testing it with early Houston classes—I was operating on all cylinders, and the progress was all that we could have hoped for. But as the organization grew, I became more and more bogged down in detail. Prior to 1983, we were in the creative stage, enrolling people in the project and creating the program. It was more fun than anything else and acted as a counterpoint to the difficult job of fundraising. But when we started delivering programs, selecting fellows, and learning how to open up new chapters, it became different for me. There were more and more management decisions—logistics, hiring people, terminating people, meeting payroll, juggling all the little details, and on and on.

About that time, I also began to realize that I was in the midst of something bigger than I was. All during the formative stages, the journey had seemed almost easy. I was swept up in the vision and the aesthetic beauty of creating the Leadership Forum. At some point, however, when all of the people were assembled and the work was being done, I "woke up" and realized what was happening. I had gathered all of these people—the trustees, the founders, the consultants, the funders, and my partners in the American Leadership Forum and the Executive

Ventures Group, the division we had created to deliver the part of the program that took place in the wilderness. To me, the payroll was huge, the expectations were huge, and the task seemed almost overwhelming. The pressure was on to produce. Who did I think I was? What was I doing here in the midst of all of this? I felt a great deal of anxiety, and I began questioning my ability to carry the whole thing off. It was like the time I almost made a perfect score skeet shooting and "woke up" only to miss the last target.

The sense of true freedom and clarity of purpose I had experienced in the early days after returning from London began to erode. I was being forced to operate at a pace I found uncomfortable. I do best when I have plenty of time to reflect on things, and "process" what's going on. That's the way I stay anchored in the midst of the necessary chaos. That was fine in the early days, when the pace was less frenetic. But now I wasn't able to control the pace and the more I operated at the others' pace, the less clear and coherent I could be about my internal direction.

In this process, I failed to follow through on some of the really important opportunities presented to me. For example, David Bohm wrote a note to me early in 1983 saying how much he enjoyed our meeting a couple of years earlier. He hoped we could get together again for further dialogue. It's indescribably painful for me to look back on this missed opportunity, but at that time I felt there were too many obligations and responsibilities at home. So I put it on the back burner and later failed to follow up. As I look back now, this was a manifestation of an incompleteness in me. Of all things, the most important for me was to continue to understand the principles that Bohm and I had talked about in London—to be able to begin to apply them in the real situations that I was encountering. I needed the spiritual nourishment and direction Bohm could have provided, but I was too blinded by the day-to-day responsibilities to see the opportunity being handed to me.

This incompleteness in me also resulted in my attracting some key people around me on whom I ultimately couldn't rely—people whose deepest interest was not in the Forum, but in their own agendas.

In one extreme case, a key player undermined the entire process we had underway for opening a chapter in a large metropolitan community in the Northeast. She and the potential executive director for the new chapter devised an alternative program which they planned to deliver under the auspices of a different organization at a substantial personal gain to themselves. This program was in direct conflict with her responsibility at the Forum, and although the problem was eventually solved, the whole affair resulted in substantial loss of time, energy, and momentum at a critical period.

This was an unusual case. But there were others which in their own ways caused equally significant degrees of incoherence in the organization. These included senior headquarters staff, and some who had critical roles at the community level. They were hard-working, well-intentioned people who felt they were contributing something important to the effort. Yet there was this underlying incoherence, and there seemed to be no way to deal with it. We struggled and struggled with it, but under these circumstances, the flow never continues. The effortless nature of the enterprise disappears, and everything becomes struggle and strain and hard work. The incoherence was so deep at one point that it ultimately resulted in our dissolving the division that delivered our wilderness program. Thinking back on this kind of incoherence, I can only say that it was like waking up behind enemy lines. I felt deeply uncomfortable, as if I was not a true member of my own community. It was a highly distressing experience for me.

It's so easy under these circumstances to blame the situation on others: "They simply don't get it. . . . They're not committed," or such. There's always a "they." But that's where the confusion lies. In these situations, it's not "they" who are responsible. It's us. It has to do with our own history being evoked. Our history of separation, isolation, low self-esteem, and unworthiness interacts with our new awareness of incoherence and creates a movie in our head that points to "them" and the problem.

What's the way out of this trap? Leaving doesn't solve anything, because usually we will end up with other people who "just don't get it." It means recognizing that if we're working with people who don't get it, it's because part of our own history is being evoked, and there's real inner work to do in addition to outer work.

The key to overcoming the trap of overactivity is in doing the inner, reflective work, individually and collectively necessary to regain our balance. In the heat of the creative process, we end up having so much to do that we lose the necessary orientation to stay in the flow. Unless we have the individual and collective discipline to continually stay anchored, we will eventually lose the flow.

That's why the discipline of dialogue seems to be so important for everyone in such an enterprise. Taking the time to come together on a regular basis in true dialogue gives everyone a chance to maintain a reflective space at the heart of the activity—a space where all people can continue to be re-nurtured *together* by what is wanting to happen, to unfold. It must be a regular discipline, and it must continue throughout the life of the undertaking, because the purpose of the enterprise will continue to evolve. The re-nurturing must take place in the midst of and as a part of that evolution. It is an essential element of the unfolding.

⊱┄◈┄◦┄◈┄⊰

Looking back at this aspect of my experience with the Forum is painful for me. I see the people I hurt and might have served better but for my ignorance. I made so many mistakes, and I'm ashamed that I was not more aware, more capable. It's difficult to come to grips with this, yet I know this was all an essential part of my development, my own unfolding. A crucial part of our life's journey is the struggle to overcome our accumulated baggage in order to ultimately operate in the flow of the unfolding generative order. The only way to accomplish this is to literally go through it—to encounter the traps and learn from them. That experience is priceless.

18. THE POWER OF COMMITMENT

This is the true joy in life, the being used for a purpose recognized by
yourself as a mighty one . . . the being a force of nature instead of a feverish,
selfish little clod of ailments and grievances complaining that the world
will not devote itself to making you happy.
—George Bernard Shaw

In early 1988, we were in the midst of opening a new Forum chapter in Silicon Valley, California. I had been away for the entire week, but returned to Houston on Friday in time to take Mavis to the Museum of Fine Arts for the opening of a new show. We were among the last few to leave that night. We had parked the car a block or so away on a dark, unlit street lined with trees. When we walked out of the museum, it was raining, and so I suggested that Mavis stay in front, and I would bring the car back for her. When I reached our car, I opened the door, folded up my umbrella and threw it into the back seat, and slipped behind the wheel. Just as I was about to close the door, I felt cold steel in my ribs.

I looked up, and there was a large man, about twenty-five years old, with a fierce look on his face, holding a bayonet-sized knife against my ribs. He wasn't just holding it there, he was pressing it hard into my ribs and saying through clenched teeth, "I don't want to hurt you, but I will. Now you move over from behind that steering wheel."

I took my key and held it up to him and said, "Just take the car and let me out." He jammed the knife into my ribs again harder and said, "I don't want the car, I want you."

I don't know what he wanted, but I felt I was a dead man if I moved over. I glanced to my right and saw another man standing right outside the door on the passenger side. I remember thinking for an instant, I'm *not* going to let this man kill me. I'm doing something too important, and I've got to finish it. With that, I grabbed his wrist with both hands before he could shove the knife any further into me, and I pulled it away, slamming his hand against the door jamb, and causing the knife to fall on the ground. In that instant I was able to swing my feet around outside and hold them up as barriers. By that time, he had the knife again and began thrusting and trying to slash through my feet. I remember kicking him in the face, landing a powerful blow. He backed off with the knife in his hand and was ready to come at me again when I began yelling at him at the top of my voice. He had the knife in his hand, thrust out toward me, and he was ready to come at me, and I screamed at him, "You dirty son of a bitch, you touch me again and I'll kill you, I'll kill you with my bare hands, God damn you! Come on, come on, just try it!"

He took a step backward and looked. I screamed even louder, "Come on, you filthy son of a bitch." I felt like a crazed animal. He stood there and looked at me for what seemed like a long while and then turned away and ran, and his partner ran with him. As he ran away, I was still screaming at him at the top of my lungs.

When they were gone, and as I was trying to collect myself, I began realizing what had happened. As the adrenaline wore down, the fear set in, and I started to shake uncontrollably. At that moment I didn't know much about the process of what had happened there, but I knew I had felt within me the power to defend myself with my bare hands against that huge knife. The reason I had felt this power was my commitment to what I had undertaken. My purpose was to bring the American Leadership Forum to life, and this person was not going to stop that. The commitment to the Leadership Forum went past mere intention—I was one with the cause.

This was a defining moment in my life, one I've considered many times. At that moment, when I realized my life's calling was in danger, suddenly a primal part of me came into play. It was as if I became a force of nature, so strong that life could not be taken from me. It was pure energy which I had not had access to previously. Out of this experience I came to understand more about the nature of the commitment necessary to actively participate in the unfolding generative order.

There are two aspects of commitment. There is a commitment to take action, which is symbolically represented, for instance, by my leaving the firm. How do you know people are committed? Because they are taking action. They are crossing the threshold of adventure, and this is the necessary first step toward the inner transformation Greenleaf spoke about. This is the kind of action we ordinarily speak of in business and in management circles.

This was my real forte. I had been taught by the Colonel from the earliest days about commitment and discipline. "If you really want to succeed at trial practice, be prepared to outwork your adversary. That's the key." I knew all about that kind of commitment, the will to stick with something you've started to the very end. "Do it right and don't let anything get in your way."

But there is a second more subtle aspect to commitment and will, and that is the *ground of being* for taking action. My appreciation of this second aspect of commitment had begun to crystallize in my meeting with Bohm and developed over the ensuing years.

What is the ground of being that allowed me to take action in a way that was consonant with my overall quest? What was the ground of being that allowed the synchronicity to occur—meeting Bohm himself, meeting Mavis, and the "moments of swing" that had occurred over the months that followed? The nature of my commitment shifted when my ground of being shifted. It was a different type of commitment, a different base for taking action. It's what Martin Buber called the "grand will" as opposed to the "puny, unfree will":

> The free man is he who wills without arbitrary self-will.
>
> He believes in destiny, and believes that it stands in need of him. It does not keep him in leading-strings, it awaits him, he must go to it, yet does not know where it is to be found. But he knows that he must go out with his whole being. The matter will not turn out according to his decision; but what is to come will come only when he decides on what he is able to will. He must sacrifice his puny, unfree will, that is controlled by things and instincts, to his grand will, which quits defined for destined being. Then, he intervenes no more, but at the same time he does not let things merely happen. He listens to what is emerging from himself, to the course of being in the world; not in order to be supported by it, but in order to bring it to reality as it desires.

The ground of being that enables the grand will to operate is the ground of being of the implicate order—being a part of the unfolding process of the universe, "the course of being in the world." It manifests in our living our life by doing, by taking action now. We are more certain of the direction than the goal, and each day we ask for guidance to take the next step. We devote our life to doing what we need to do— really need to do—each day. We pay attention to all that is going on around us. Our awareness operates at multiple levels, and we listen carefully with all we have for what to do next. We never see the whole landscape, so we take the next tiny step and improvise on what we've learned. This thought is captured beautifully by the Spanish poet A. Machado: "Wanderer, there is no path. You lay a path in walking." This is a very different kind of commitment—and it's at the heart of the inner transformation that Greenleaf spoke about.

There is a paradox at work here. From our old perspective, "grand will" sounds as if we're asking someone else to tell us what to do. But something important has shifted—and what has fundamentally shifted is the "I." I am making up my own mind, but my sense of identity has shifted. I am now part of the unfolding, generative process, and in this state of being, I am no longer controlled by things and instincts.

In this state of being, we will do things that are very difficult, and which might even be unnatural for us in terms of our habitual way of doing things. In this new commitment we take on major challenges, seemingly impossible challenges, and we work extremely hard and stay totally focused—yet it's not a struggle. In fact, it's "effortless."

When I walked away from that meeting with Bohm, the need to give birth to the Leadership Forum began to grow as an all-consuming purpose in my life. It gave my life meaning. It was my life, and I was it. It was my destiny. And it was as if I had no further choice. I felt exactly the way Carl Jung described himself:

> I had a sense of destiny as though my life was assigned to me by fate and had to be fulfilled. This gave me an inner security. . . . Often I had the feeling that in all decisive matters, I was no longer among men, but was alone with God.

As I look back on it, it was almost irrational, because the dream was so large. I didn't really know what I was doing at the time. I had no contacts in the field of leadership development, I didn't have the necessary seed money, and I didn't have any idea how I was going to accomplish what I felt I had to do. Yet I had this inner knowing that despite all of those obstacles, I would fulfill my dream.

For the longest time I was fearless, like the warrior Joseph Campbell describes going into battle. I stopped being swayed by other people's opinions, I stopped worrying about what my colleagues and neighbors would think, and I found a new force within me.

From the moment I walked out of Bohm's office, what happened to me had the most mysterious quality about it. Things began falling into place almost effortlessly—unforeseen incidents and meetings with the most remarkable people who were to provide crucial assistance to me.

This was the implicate order at work in my life. The experience of the generative order operating through your life is an exhilarating experience—as if you are riding the crest of a wave.

One of the clearest expressions of this experience I've seen came during the dialogue between Bill Moyers and Joseph Campbell which resulted in the six-hour PBS television series based on Campbell's writings, *The Power of Myth*:

> MOYERS: Do you ever have this sense when you are following your bliss, as I have at moments, of being helped by hidden hands?
>
> CAMPBELL: All the time. It's miraculous. I even have a superstition that has grown on me as the result of invisible hands coming all the time— namely, that if you do follow your bliss, you put yourself on a kind of track that has been there all the while, waiting for you, and the life that you ought to be living is the one you are living. When you can see that, you begin to meet people who are in the field of your bliss, and they open the doors to you. I say, follow your bliss and don't be afraid, and doors will open where you didn't know they were going to be.

PART FOUR

THE GIFT

⊱──◦──⊰

Until one is committed there is hesitancy,
the chance to draw back, always ineffectiveness.

Concerning all acts of initiative (and creation)
there is one elementary truth, the ignorance of which
kills countless ideas and splendid plans:

The moment one definitely commits oneself,
then Providence moves too.

All sorts of things occur to help one that would otherwise
never have occurred. A whole stream of events issues from the decision,
raising in one's favor all manner of unforeseen incidents and
meetings and material assistance,
which no man could have dreamed would have come his way.

—W. N. Murray, *The Scottish Himalayan Expedition*

19. THE RETURN—AND VENTURING FORTH AGAIN

The incident outside the museum was a watershed in my life. It brought to my immediate attention the power of the principles that had been at play over the past eight years. By this time, my life was a series of connections with people. Making these synchronous connections had become a natural way of operating; in fact, I was unable to operate any other way. I began learning how to move *with* the unfolding order and to live out the principles, naturally.

Over time, I developed more sensitivity to the inner voice that was speaking to me. I found that I needed to have plenty of reflective time in order to allow the principles to operate. I did this by running early in the morning and taking time during the day, whenever I could, to reflect and listen. When I did, I found the attractiveness principle starting to operate on a regular basis in my life. In some ways, for me, it was an amazing state to live in. I had to do my work, treating it as my ultimate concern, and then simply wait expectantly in the warrior repose with acute awareness for the opportune moment—the "cubic centimeter of chance." When the opportunity presented itself, I was required to move instantly without conscious premeditation.

Many times I didn't fully understand the moves I made in this state until later. Very slight, deft movements at just the right time and place would have enormous consequences. Timing was crucial. When that moment came, with just the slightest gesture, all sorts of actions and results were brought into being. This is the principle of *economy of means* that is in evidence more and more as we learn to operate with real mastery in life.

A seemingly insignificant encounter I had just a few weeks after the incident at the museum is a good illustration of this principle. This thirty-second conversation set in motion a whole train of events that formed the entire next stage of my life.

One evening I attended a meeting of the Houston Lyceum, a group of about two dozen business and professional people from the Houston area who would meet for a couple of hours over dinner every two months to exchange ideas and learn together. Usually, the member responsible for the program brought in an interesting personality to engage in conversation with the members. On this occasion, in February 1988, a member invited Norman Duncan to explain to us the process of scenario planning used by the Royal Dutch Shell Group of companies. I had met Norm Duncan a time or two prior to this occasion, and I knew him to be a highly respected executive at Shell Oil Company, one of the Shell Group's largest subsidiaries. He reported directly to the Chief Executive Officer. Norm told us that evening that instead of relying on forecasts (which are invariably wrong), the Shell Group does its planning for the future through the use of decision scenarios. Scenario planning, he said, is not about making plans, but is the process whereby management teams change their mental models of the business environment and the world. In the Shell Group, scenario planning is a trigger to institutional learning. A manager's inner model never mirrors reality, he explained—it's always a construct. The scenario process is aimed at these perceptions inside the mind of a decision maker. By presenting other ways of seeing the world, decision scenarios give managers something very precious: the ability to re-perceive reality, leading to strategic insights beyond the mind's reach.

The team of scenario planners in London, Norm said, included experts in economics, sociopolitics, energy, the environment, and technology. They conduct ongoing conversations with fifty or so top managers in the Shell Group and with a network of remarkable, leading-edge thinkers from around the world in many disciplines: politics, science, education, business, economics, technology, religion, and the arts. Every three years or so, they synthesize this information into two or more scenarios—stories about how the business might evolve over the coming years and decades. Considering these scenarios and their consequences provides the foundation for the Shell Group's approach to strategic management.

We were all fascinated by Norm's presentation. A number of the business leaders commented that this approach to strategic management had, in large part, led the

Shell Group to be regarded as one of the best-managed companies in the world. The conversation that evening was lively and animated, and it lasted far longer than was intended. At the close of the conversation, Norm commented that he had been asked to join the scenario team in London to help develop and produce their current round of scenarios. He would be leaving in two weeks.

As everyone else was gathering their things to leave, I just sat there for a moment, digesting what I had heard. Then spontaneously I went over to Norm and told him how absorbing I had found his presentation and how I admired him for being selected for that new post. "Boy, would I love to do something like that sometime," I commented. Norm smiled and thanked me. With that we shook hands, I wished him luck, and we were off in our separate directions.

It was about ten months later, in December 1988, that I received a telephone call one morning from Renata Karlin, a representative in New York of the Royal Dutch Shell Group of companies. She was calling to make an appointment to see me, but didn't explain the purpose of her visit. I assumed it was about our program and the support that Shell Oil Company, the Group's U.S. subsidiary, had been giving us over the years.

When we met in my office a week later, Ms. Karlin got straight to the point. She asked whether I would be willing to be considered, along with others, for a four-year assignment as the head of the Group's worldwide scenario planning team in London. I was completely taken aback by her suggestion and told her so. We talked at length about the proposal, and I promised I would get back to her within a week.

That evening, when Mavis and I got home from work and the kids were in bed, we sat down to talk. I was excited about what had been presented—a real gift and an opportunity to learn that was unparalleled in scope. Yet, our personal life was so complex. In a way, it didn't make sense even to discuss the possibility of moving to London. Mavis was in the midst of her residency at Baylor College of Medicine. She had made a real mark there and loved what she was doing. The very last thing that would ever cross our minds was her leaving the program. It just wasn't in our scheme of things.

Furthermore, we had just finished building a large new home in Houston near the Texas Medical Center. In three years Mavis would set up her practice there. We had spent over two years planning, designing, and building that home. We had been in it for less than nine months, and we had both vowed never to move again.

So when I began telling Mavis of Renata Karlin's proposal, I was in a really conflicted state. On the one hand, I was being offered an opportunity that was right at the center of my interests. Yet at that moment, my highest priority was to help Mavis fulfill her dream to become a physician. Everything else was secondary.

In the midst of telling Mavis the story, she smiled at me knowingly. I was puzzled and stopped in the middle of a sentence. Then she broke into a big grin and said: "I told you so—remember, in front of St. Paul's Cathedral?" I drew a quick breath. It was true. Five years earlier Mavis and I had taken a trip to London where I had showed her all of my old haunts that I had told her so much about: my law office in Grosvenor Square, my flat where I had first read about David Bohm that Sunday morning, my favorite restaurants and parks, and little streets in Chelsea that I loved to visit while walking and thinking about things.

One evening Mavis and I had taken a taxi to St. Paul's Cathedral. Just as we began walking up the steps of the cathedral, Mavis stopped and took me by the arm and said: "Joseph, I want you to know something I am certain of. In the next few years you will move back to London with the family and me. You'll be doing important work for a very large multinational company." At that point, I was in the midst of forming the Hartford Chapter for the Forum, so her words seemed too farfetched to take seriously. Also, at that stage in our relationship, I hadn't yet learned to take Mavis's premonitions as seriously as I do now.

From the instant Mavis reminded me of her premonition in front of St. Paul's, she took the lead in the conversation. She said it was our destiny to go. She said there was nothing to question about it. She said ALF was moving from a startup to a more operational phase of its life. It had always been my intention to turn things over to more capable operational hands when that point had been reached. "Besides," she reminded me, "you always said your ultimate intent was to take the ALF principles and apply them globally. This is your chance to learn more about how you can do that. It's all part of the larger scheme of things." The conversation from that point on centered around the possibilities presented to us—how we would arrange our lives and affairs "when," as Mavis put it, this assignment was offered to me. This turn in the conversation was completely contrary to what I had expected. But Mavis simply said, "It's what's meant to happen. It's obviously the thing to do."

In view of the involved nature of our personal lives at that time, the discussion around this sort of issue could have been horribly difficult—trade-offs, negotiating individual situations, hand-wringing about leaving the house. Yet the decision to go for it was made that evening in very short order. All of the other issues were subordinated at that moment to what was meant to happen.

Mavis and I talked about following our inner voice, the voice that helps us to understand what is wanting to manifest in the world, and we reminisced about the lessons that she and I learned together over the years about following that intuition. Mavis has always been anchored in this way of being—attuned to her inner voice and her inner capacity for high perception and precognition. This way of being comports with life in the bubble chamber, where time-space processes sometimes run in reverse causal sequences, and notions of earlier and later are no longer clear.

Over the years these incidences of Mavis's precognition occurred on a regular basis. I came to accept them as a way of life and usually didn't think much about them. When I had been in London with the Shell Group for about two years, Mavis and I were rushing down a hotel corridor on the way to a meeting when she pulled at my arm and stopped me. She turned to me and simply said: "We'll be living in Boston when you complete your assignment at Shell." Of course we had never even thought about Boston. Our game plan was to return to Houston and to pick up where we had left off. But I guess it goes without saying that at this moment, almost three years later, with my assignment at Shell completed, I'm writing these words at our home in the North Shore of Boston.

>-+-◆>-○-<◆-+-<

As I traveled around to the chapters during those final months, I found much to celebrate in the Forum. In meetings with the senior fellows—the amalgam of classes that had graduated in prior years—I saw one of the most visible results of the work we had done: the extraordinary high energy of coherence among such diverse groups. In those settings, I could feel their collective mind at work. Sometimes at those meetings national figures would come to sit in dialogue with the fellows— people like Jack Kemp and Warren Bennis and John Gardner. They would consistently comment to me about this high energy of coherence and the love among the fellows. This coherence and love are still characteristic of ALF, which continues to flourish long after my departure.

The final months before I left ALF were also a time of deep reflection about the events of my life since the beginning of the Forum in 1980. What had occurred during those years was in itself a representation of the generative order. The generative process is a continual unfolding, and we are here to participate in it. In fact, we are most deeply satisfied when we are participating in that creative process, whether through being a parent, forming an organization, or working on a project.

In looking back, I thought about the birth of our son, Leon, in 1982 and our daughter, Shannon, four years later. The joy and wonder I experienced then are beyond words. I participated in those births as a full partner, sadly unlike when Joey was born during my earlier life.

When Leon was born, the doctor gave him immediately to Mavis, who was fully awake, having given birth naturally without the aid of anesthetics. He suckled on her breast for a minute or so, and then he was given over to me. That little infant, smeared from head to toe with the remnants of his world in his mother's womb, was screaming with his eyes shut against the bright light. I took him gently and began to place him in the warm water of the Leboyer bath. As I did, I spoke softly to him, just as I had each night when he was in the womb: "Leon, this is Daddy—your old pal. Don't worry little fella, it's all going to be all right." As I spoke, he abruptly stopped crying, opened his little eyes for the first time, and looked straight into mine. In that instant our souls connected. He clearly recognized the sound of my voice. With tears streaming down my face, I placed Leon into the warm bathwater to wash him and comfort him. As I did so, he kept looking straight into my eyes, not uttering a sound, just relaxing in my hands as I continued to speak gently to him. This moment of our connection for the first time in the "outside world" will remain forever.

The connection with my son was one of the real gifts my years with ALF had given me because ALF was itself an expression of my own development as a person. As the years passed, I learned more about myself and what my real priorities were. My marriage to Mavis, the bonding experience with Leon at his birth, and later with Shannon at hers, are three gifts of unspeakable importance that came my way in this unfolding process.

There's one more, though, that is just as important. That gift grew out of the discipline of journal writing that I learned to appreciate more deeply during the development of our wilderness curriculum.

As a result of the work I was doing with my journal, I began to recognize some of the anger I had towards the Colonel. So one day I went to him in the living room of the ranch and said, "Colonel, I don't think you've ever told me you love me. I believe you do love me, but why haven't you ever told me so?"

He just kept quiet. He didn't know what to say. After a while he looked down and said, "Well, you know I love you."

And I said, "Well, why can't you tell me?"

He said, "I've always loved you, and you know I have. You know I love you."

I said, "I don't know it, and it hurts that you never told me so."

Then, as we got ready to go our separate ways, I just put my arms around him and hugged him real hard and held him. He was stiff as a board. There was no response from him at all. He was rigid. I held him and patted him on the back and said good-bye.

I imagine the Colonel wasn't expressive about love because his father never told him that he loved him. He came from the old school, where to say "I love you" to another male was just not a manly thing to do. A man was always in control. A man never wept or cried. A man took care of everything, particularly in his family, and was the authority figure in the house. In the older paradigm that my father came from, the man was a little set apart from the rest of the family. He showed his manliness by being tough—tough-minded and tough-willed, never admitting he didn't know. Expressing emotion was not part of that picture.

I kept on hugging my father whenever we met, and gradually, over the next year or so, he began to come back to me when we said good-bye so I could hold him. Eventually, it came about that every time we said hello, and every time we said good-bye, he would give me a great big bear hug. He also got comfortable enough to say, "I love you." Our whole relationship became more expressive.

During this time, the Colonel established a kind of tradition between the two of us. Each Friday we would meet together for lunch at the Coronado Club in Houston. These Friday lunches meant so much to me that I now carry on the tradition with my son Joey whenever I am in Houston, which currently is quite often. Joey is a highly regarded trial lawyer there, establishing quite a name for himself. He and I have learned over the years, with a lot of hard work, how to build a loving and healthy father-son relationship, and today I consider that relationship as one of my most important treasures.

➤━◆➤━○━◆━┥◄

One Friday at lunch the Colonel looked at me and said, "Bud, when I die, I want to die with my boots on, chopping cedar at the ranch." We got up to go, and as we were leaving, we hugged one another good-bye. It was very natural; it wasn't a big deal. Just two days later, while clearing a hillside at the ranch, he died of a heart attack.

I keep thinking what it would have been like for me if we had never made this transition, if we had never really learned to express our love for one another. I wonder what it would have been like had I just shaken hands with him that day at the Coronado Club, and he had turned around, and I had never seen him again.

20. SETTING THE FIELD

I arrived in London in mid-April 1990, a time of astonishing change in the world. Just a few months earlier, the Berlin Wall had abruptly crumbled. The Soviet Union had also collapsed, and with it, the assumptions and framework of international affairs since the Second World War. It was a time of great excitement and anticipation, and I felt certain it was right for me to be in this place at this particular time.

I had undergone an intensive screening process over the four months following my initial contact with Renata Karlin, making several trips to London and the Hague where I had met with many of the senior officers in the Royal Dutch Shell Group. During this process, I spent a significant amount of time with the Planning Coordinator, Arie de Geus, to whom Karlin reported, and in the final stage of the process, I spent the better part of a day in the Hague with the Chairman and Deputy Chairman of the Group.

I had done a significant amount of homework over the intervening months since I had first been contacted by Shell. I had read everything I could put my hands on about the Shell Group and its processes of scenario planning. I felt comfortable with the concept of planning through the means of scenarios, expecially because I felt that it would never again be possible for business and governments to effectively "plan" a long-term future. Instead, it was necessary to learn to create and discover an unfolding future. I could see how the Shell process of scenario planning fit right into the center of the quantum view of the universe that Bohm had described to me so long ago. It was all consonant with the way I had begun to operate in my own life.

All matter and the universe are continually in motion. At a level we cannot see, there is an unbroken wholeness, an "implicate order" out of which seemingly discrete events arise. All human beings are part of that unbroken whole which is continually unfolding. One of our responsibilities in life is to be open and learn, thereby becoming more capable of sensing and actualizing emerging new realities.

Now I felt that I was being given an opportunity to learn more about this process but on a vastly larger scale, in an organization with over 120,000 employees operating in more than one hundred countries worldwide. Moreover, my inner voice was saying that this was an important opportunity to begin to learn how these principles might be applied on a global scale outside the realm of the corporation itself. This seemed to be part of what was unfolding for me—the opportunity to begin to learn about positively influencing and shaping global events rather than simply accepting and reacting to the larger forces that were at play.

It may have seemed grandiose, even foolish to think in such large terms and, being mindful of this, I was careful about what I said about these feelings and to whom I said it. Yet my understanding of the way the universe works led me to believe that this kind of learning was not just possible, but imperative if the world was going to successfully navigate the turbulent times ahead.

Among large corporations, it seemed to me that Royal Dutch Shell was unique in somehow being able, with remarkable regularity, to tap into the very best thinking about the future. I hoped to better understand exactly how the scenario process really worked and how it might be developed further. As early as 1972, Shell scenarios envisaged the formation of OPEC and the sudden oil price shock that hit in the winter 1973-1974, just as they foresaw the equally significant oil price collapse that began in January 1986. In 1984, a proprietary Shell regional scenario, dubbed "The Greening of Russia," described a possible breakup of the Soviet Union and the ensuing chaos in Eastern Europe. What interested me most was not just the accuracy of these stories, but the way the scenario process might help people to better perceive complex realities and to shape the future, not only within, but beyond the corporation itself.

I was aware, for example, of the significant impact the Shell scenario process had made in South Africa in recent years. A scenario team which included former Shell scenario chief Pierre Wack was formed in the early 1980s in South Africa. Supported by the Anglo-American Mining Corporation, the team had seen a "high road" and a "low road" in South Africa's future. Starting around 1985, presentations based on the team's work were made to government officials, business leaders, black community groups, and groups of exiled black leaders. These presentations engaged thousands of people in thinking about the choices ahead. Either apartheid could be dismantled, and the country could develop an open political and economic system and reenter the world community, or apartheid could continue, with the country experiencing increasing isolation, economic stagnation, and internal strife. The remarkable developments that became evident publicly at the time of de Klerk's historic speech in February 1990 and that have continued to unfold to this day had, in many important respects, their roots in the discovery by the South African people that the course they were on was unsustainable and that they had a choice about their future.

I continued to think about Bell's theorem and my meeting with Bohm, which had forever changed my view of how the universe is linked together by a fabric of invisible connections. I realized that small changes at just the right place can have a systemwide impact because these changes share the unbroken wholeness that unites the entire system. A seemingly insignificant act in one part of the whole creates nonlocal results that emerge far away. Unseen connections create effects at a distance—"quantum leaps"—in places quite surprising to us. This model of change comported with my daily experience much more so than the traditional model of incremental change.

I was aware scientists had begun to speak of "fields" to explain the connections that they observed. Bohm had mentioned the "general fielding" for all mankind when we met together in London. "We are all connected and operate within living fields of thought and perception," he had said to me.

Just a few months prior to moving to London for this assignment, I had an opportunity to learn more about this new type of field theory from a prominent British biologist, Rupert Sheldrake. Sheldrake and I were guests of a mutual friend whose home was in Santa Fe, New Mexico. I spent the weekend absorbed in conversation with him and walked away from that encounter with a deeper understanding of the phenomenon of dialogue, of how the universe is interconnected, and of how my work at Shell might contribute on a wider basis.

Fields, Sheldrake said, are nonmaterial regions of influence—invisible forces that structure space or behavior. The earth's gravitational field, for example, is all around us. We cannot see it, it's not a material object, but it's nevertheless real. It gives things weight and makes things full. There are also magnetic fields that underlie the functioning of our brains and bodies. Countless vibratory patterns of activity occur within these fields which we can't detect with our senses, but which can be tuned into radio and TV receivers. "Although the nature of fields is inevitably mysterious, we take all of this for granted," he told me. There are also, he said, fundamental quantum matter fields recognized by physicists—electron fields, neutron fields, and others. They are "invisible, intangible, inaudible, tasteless, and odorless," and yet in quantum theory, they are the substance of the universe. Fields are states of space, but space is full of energy and invisible structures that interconnect.

As we spoke, I couldn't help but think of the energy field that I experienced consistently there in Santa Fe, particularly at the home of Charles and Beth Miller, where we were staying that weekend. Over the years, I had often come to the Millers' home (which was also the artist Georgia O'Keeffe's former residence, Sol y Sombra), to write and think and learn by engaging in deep conversation with the remarkable people who gathered there. I could literally feel the field forming whenever I was there—like my experiences at the cathedral at Chartres, or on backpacking trips in the wilderness, or in the dialogues around the campfire during the Leadership Forum wilderness experience, and even on the racetrack at Monza.

The time spent with Sheldrake gave me a deeper appreciation for the possibilities of dialogue and of large systems change. As a result of this encounter, I began to see more clearly the importance of dialogue and organizational learning for the process by which humans might govern themselves.

At the outset of my assignment with Shell, all of this was at the forefront of my mind. For four months I lived alone in London while Mavis completed her first year of residency for medical school. This gave me the time I needed to get completely grounded in the work I intended to do. I spent all of my time alone reading and thinking, considering both the immediate and the larger purpose of the work I was undertaking. For many years I had followed the discipline of preparing the personal choices and fundamental goals I sought to accomplish for the coming year. I wrote these down and, on a regular basis, painted pictures in my mind of what I had chosen to do. At the top of the list I prepared in January 1990 was to create for Royal Dutch Shell a set of global scenarios that would begin the process of positively shaping and influencing collective thought, not only in Shell, but in the world at large—scenarios that would help ensure social cohesion in a world of increasing fragmentation. My commitment was to do all that was within my power to accomplish this and, in that process, to trust nature that whatever was needed would become available to me.

In order to accomplish this goal, I knew I had to develop these scenarios collectively with the most diverse and knowledgeable scenario team I could put together. These scenarios could not be developed by me alone with a support staff feeding information to me. Rather, these scenarios would have to be developed through the collective wisdom of the entire unit. Diversity on the team was a prime objective, and I immediately focused on accomplishing that objective.

A number of the players were already on board, but others, both from inside and outside Shell, were left to recruit. We ultimately had people on the team from Japan, Singapore, Africa, Canada, the United States, Australia, the Netherlands, France, England, and Scotland. We had good luck in the recruitment process, but we missed on the people we tried to locate and recruit from South America, India, and China.

With the team assembled, I set about doing what I could to help set the field— that is, to set the space within our organization by articulating the values we held, what we considered important, how we interacted among ourselves, and how we would interact with the rest of the Group. We instituted a process that enabled us to stay in constant conversation with one another. This included regular debriefing sessions, luncheon learning sessions, a constant stream of interesting outside speakers, and regular "away days" for the entire team to learn together and to reconnect with one another.

The first task was to set the vision for our team and for how we were to operate. I was gratified at the overall coherence of the group that I saw from the outset. There was high energy on this team—this was a group of highly intelligent people hand-picked from all the disciplines represented in the Group. The balance, about 20 percent, were recruited from the outside. These were all "racehorses" who knew the import and value to the Group of the work we were to undertake, and who were proud to be on this select team.

I was struck, however, from the very outset at how rational the Westerners in the group seemed to be, and how skeptical and even disdainful most of them were of anything that smacked of what they referred to as "the soft stuff"—anything that could not be measured or quantified. Graphs and charts were the order of the day because quantification and measurement were what was seen as real. This was very difficult for me because over the previous ten years or so, I had come to see the immeasurable as precisely that which was most real, that which I cared most deeply about. I recalled what Bohm had said about this: "The attempt to suppose that measure exists prior to man and independently of him leads, as has been seen, to the 'objectification' of man's insight so that it becomes rigidified and unable to change, eventually bringing about fragmentation and general confusion."

I felt like a fish out of water a great deal of the time during these early days. On the other hand, I knew this was a blessing to me, because I needed this kind of exposure to give me the capacity and balance to handle such encounters effectively in the future. This was part of the reason I was here, part of my learning. And I did have an immense amount to learn in a very short period of time. So from the outset I became an open system, listening, absorbing, asking questions, and understanding all I could about the business of the Shell Group worldwide, about how it was managed, and about its unique corporate culture. This process was greatly enhanced by the scenario interview process I began early on in my assignment.

Over the following six months I met with some fifty or so of the Group's senior management, including the managing directors, regional and functional coordinators, and CEOs of the most important Shell operating companies worldwide. I spent three very intense hours, sometimes more, locked away with these managers in one-on-one conversations. They understood exactly why I was there—to uncover their mental models of the external and internal environment of Shell, the first step in developing global scenarios for the Group. It was a fascinating experience and absolutely the best process for building relationships and familiarizing me with the overall culture of the Group. Many of these conversations rose to the level of dialogue or close to it. They were rich with meaning. All of the hallmarks were there—the flow, the unusual coherence, and the sense of collective wisdom arising from the encounters. And in this process I met a number of people who were clearly like family—people I knew I could count on for resources, connections, and support whenever I needed help as my work unfolded.

Out of this process, it was our tentative conclusion that the global scenarios for the next thirty years should principally revolve around the issue of the relationships between the rich and poor countries of the world. We went to work testing our ideas and doing intense research on key issues. We assigned "building blocks" to small project teams who were to research and develop issues and then report back to the whole group in three-day plenary sessions that we held offsite.

Over the next twelve months, members of our team fanned out all over the world doing "on the ground" research. We began with the emerging countries, including Argentina, Brazil, Mexico, India, China, the newly industrializing countries of southeast Asia, Russia, South Africa, and the Middle East. We also spent a lot of time in the industrialized countries, especially the United States, Canada, Japan, and European countries. In this process, we met the most remarkable people imaginable. We used the considerable clout of the Royal Dutch Shell Group to open doors in these countries, putting together one- and two-day workshops with the best-informed people from all the disciplines we could find. We invited the key managers in the local operating company to attend these roundtable conversations. From these joint conversations, other doors would begin to open. At that point we would let nature take its course, leading us from one insightful person to the next.

We came away from this experience with a profoundly different view of the world than we had had going into it. We didn't yet understand all of the underlying structures and the driving forces, but we all realized that we were witnessing a moment of revolutionary change in world history. Our work over the next eight months would be to put that overarching structure in place and to tell the two compelling stories of the future that we saw forming in our minds.

21. BARRICADES

The target date for the completion of the global scenarios was September 1, 1992. On that date we were scheduled to present the scenarios to the Committee of Managing Directors, Shell's top management team, for approval, and, if approved, then for dissemination throughout the entire Shell Group of companies. This was an inviolate target date, and so from the outset we had constructed a critical path we were following. The pressure was constantly on, but by January of that year, we were still on target.

We put together a six-person editorial team representing all of the project teams and locked ourselves away for two solid weeks in a private room on the top floor of a club in central London. We had breakfast and lunch there, and we agreed no one would take telephone calls. Our task was to develop the overall architecture and broad themes of the two scenarios that we saw unfolding. At the end of these two weeks, we took our conclusion back to the whole team, presented it to them, and began the process of tearing the structure of the stories apart and putting them back together again. There was a "skunk works" atmosphere pervading the entire effort. There was high stress, yet the team was operating at peak efficiency, every member contributing more than his or her share. We then fanned out once again to check our conclusions on the ground in China, India, Latin America, and South Africa.

We returned to London in April ready to begin the difficult task of actually writing the stories. Up to this point we had been meeting regularly and communicating the details through means of memoranda, interim reports, and graphs and charts illustrating our progress. But I knew deep down that the most crucial part of the entire process would be the line-by-line writing of stories. The person chosen to write the scenarios not only had to be a topnotch wordsmith and organizer, but had to be able to mediate between the "experts" on the team, who were developing extremely strong and varying views about the scenarios. With this in mind, I asked Betty Sue Flowers, a professor at the University of Texas who had edited Joseph Campbell's *The Power of Myth*, to come to London to take on this responsibility.

From the very outset I sought to gain collective agreement on the team about the driving forces that were influencing world events. Historians write about individuals and events, but usually have no language to describe the larger fundamental forces of history—what Tolstoy called "the laws of history" in *War and Peace*. Accurately identifying these forces is a prerequisite to building durable scenario stories. More importantly, I personally felt that if we deeply understood these driving forces, we could also more easily identify leverage points for change. We could see where particular actions and change could lead to significant, enduring improvements. By understanding the overall structure, we could understand how the course of history might be altered. We worked long and hard on this fundamental aspect of the scenario-building process, and strong alignment among the team developed during our work.

Eventually, we agreed that two interrelated patterns characterized fundamental change around the world: increasing liberalization and increasing globalization. We realized we were in the midst of the first truly *global* revolution—the advent of worldwide liberalization, both political and economic. Since 1989, the world had seen the reunification of Germany, free elections and economic reform in Eastern Europe, the end of Soviet communism, accelerating opening in both China and India, and the beginning of the dismantling of apartheid in South Africa. We were also witnessing far-reaching reform in Latin America and Mexico. The message we had learned during our travels over the previous eighteen months was clear—authoritarian political systems and centrally planned economies don't work in this increasingly interconnected world. One of the reasons liberalization has spread so quickly and so widely is globalization. Knowledge about how other people live and how other societies work spreads rapidly through international travel and communication. We saw that governments would increasingly find it harder to limit what people know and to resist their demand for access to goods and for control over their own destinies. Liberalization, in turn, speeds globalization by opening and freeing flows of goods and knowledge. Globalization and liberalization were thus, for now, mutually reinforcing. We saw this as an extremely potent and powerful driving force.

But we also saw that continuing liberalization was not necessarily inevitable. There are two faces to the liberalization revolution—two opposing forces that would drive the two scenarios we saw unfolding for the world. On the one hand, liberalization offers enormous opportunities to individuals, groups, companies, and societies to improve their lives. If these opportunities are seized and if they are realized, hope and expectation will generate pressure for further economic and political change. A positive feedback loop is formed—a virtuous circle occurs.

On the other hand, liberalization can threaten many people, who fear they could lose what they presently value—their national, religious, and cultural identity; their political power; their economic position. This could lead to a growing atmosphere of fear and resistance and a resulting negative feedback loop.

We saw the world at an important turning point—what might be termed a "hinge of history." The liberalization might continue to spread into a world of rapid and unsettling change, with vast new competitive markets opening up in the developing countries. We saw this as "Scenario A," which we ultimately called "New Frontiers." On the other hand, liberalization might be resisted and restricted, resulting in a world of divisions and barriers—a world deeply divided with huge disparities in wealth, with widespread poverty, urban crime, and the disregard for the environment that inevitably accompanies desperation and hopelessness. This we dubbed "Scenario B," later called "Barricades."

The team was unanimous in its view of this underlying structure. It was also in complete agreement about the story of Barricades. Our research told us that this scenario could easily unfold in history.

THE STORY OF BARRICADES

In the instability that follows the Cold War, no visionary "new world order" develops. With problems at home, even like-minded countries cannot reach agreement. GATT talks break down, and a tension grows in the relationships between the U.S. and Japan, and between the U.S. and the European Community.

But the biggest fissure is between the rich and the poor countries of the world. The rich fear the turbulent politics of the poor world. They see its spill-over effects in refugees, lawlessness, the drug trade, and environmental damage, and they want to insulate themselves. They are repelled by what they see as alien values: for example, Islamic fundamentalism and the tribal blood-letting in the Balkans, the Caucasus, and Africa. They avert their attention inward and take steps to isolate themselves from these impoverished and disease-ridden countries.

For their part, poor-country governments are suspicious of the motives of the rich, remembering their history of colonial exploitation, gunboat diplomacy, and political destabilization. The endless portrayal of rich societies as selfish, godless, amoral, and racist creates a deep alienation. Fear and suspicion rule on both sides.

The fissure widens as the rich find ways of excluding the poor through immigration controls and restructured import regimes. The poor sometimes have to be kept out physically or repatriated, as in the late 1990s, when, according to this scenario, a fundamentalist coup in Algeria sends a flood of refugees into France. The Germans deal with the Poles and Russians, the United States with the Central Americans, and the Japanese with the Chinese and Koreans in a similar way. They learn through experience that ruthlessness works politically, just as, historically, the Italians had learned in dealing with the Albanians, and the Americans had learned with the Vietnamese and Haitian boat people. In this scenario, migration policy provides a catalyst that helps fuse the European countries together in a tight and exclusive European Union. Technology helps to marginalize the poor. Automation makes cheap labor less important, while advanced telecommunications and computer networking bind the rich of the world closer together in shared systems that exclude those who cannot afford access.

But after the turn of the century, growth among the economically isolated rich countries stagnates. There is no boost from demand in poor countries. The labor force is decreasing. Environmental and social costs reduce productivity. The aging population means that both savings rates and investment rates are low, and political special-interest groups paralyze consensus building. Consequently, deficits continue to grow.

As the liberalization revolution proceeds in poor countries, it becomes clear that distinctive national tradition and culture are much more important than was believed in the heady days of the early 1990s, when the same recipes for economic growth were indiscriminately applied in Pakistan as in Poland or Peru. Indian and Mexican reforms get some results, but in Russia and Africa, no armies of entrepreneurs are waiting to create a dynamic new business sector. Foreign investors hold back, worried about the risks and waiting for the results. In countries where politicians have promised rapid results from economic reform, people cannot understand why their living standards do not rise and why they are being asked to make sacrifices for the future by saving more.

The process is traumatic and disillusioning. Outward-oriented liberalism is not seen to bring the benefits that were expected of it. Policymakers turn to the experience of "national capitalism" seen in Japan and South Korea. The "Korean model" is particularly attractive: deregulation and privatization do not involve ceding control to foreigners or upsetting vested interests. Free trade applies to exports, but not to imports.

In some countries, this more nationalistic approach to capitalism involves a painful change of direction. In the scenario, a crackdown occurs in China when moderates become alarmed at the way dynamic Guangdong province in southern China is becoming a breeding ground for corruption, criminal gangs, and prostitution, and so throw in their lot with conservatives. Together they agree to a much more carefully regulated market system and the exclusion of morally corrupting influences from the West. Elsewhere, old models that reflect a perceived need for "indigenous solutions" are revived. The new Hindu fundamentalist government in India promises it will continue with liberalization only where this is consistent with "Indian dignity." The Russian economy is much worse even than the U.S. economy during the Great Depression. Yeltsin's doomed experiment in liberalization limps along for several more years, provoking mounting disgust at the corruption, gangsterism, greed, hardship, moral degradation, and unfairness of Western capitalism. In many societies, globalism is associated with Western intrusion and dominance. In the Islamic world, particularly, Western ideas and values are rejected as "cultural pollution." The growing influence of Islamic fundamentalism is an indirect cause of the turbulence in much of the Middle East and central Asia, and a source of constant hostility where it directly confronts Christian or Hindu cultures.

In many countries, the hopes of those wanting to make a decisive break with the past—to modernize, to see big improvements in living standards, to catch up with the West—are sadly disappointed. The tensions of perpetual frustration, manifested in organized and petty crime, political instability, and sporadic violence, are felt most acutely in the big cities of the poor world. The overall environment in many African, Latin American, and Asian countries is such that few multinational companies are interested in investing, even when governments offer big tax breaks to entice them.

In trade, as with migration, the rich erect barricades against the poor. For example, the greater concern about the environment in rich countries leads to costly regulations, which lead to a widening gap in production costs between the rich and the poor. To level the playing field in relation to poor countries that do not have such regulations, rich countries impose various "green tariffs," gradually squeezing poor-country products out of rich-country markets. For most poor countries, the avenue of export-led growth is effectively closed.

Underlying this new international order is the ability of the rich world to sustain indifference to the poor world's problems. The problems of poverty and instability in the poor world seem beyond solution. The hostility of Western electorates to aid programs, "cheap imports," and migrants from "overpopulated" neighbors is palpable. Again and again, pressing problems that require long-term solutions are met by indifference and the hasty throwing-up of barricades.

By the end of the first decade of the twenty-first century, the self-reinforcing problems of overpopulation, resource depletion, disease, and increasing lawlessness cause a tidal flow of migrants beating against the "golden curtains" of the rich. Environmental scarcity and diminishing natural resources—particularly water depletion—inflame existing hatreds. Large-scale border upheavals occur, and the poor countries become increasingly ungovernable. The distinction between war and crime in the poor countries becomes increasingly blurred, and criminal anarchy emerges as a significant strategic danger to the rich countries.

By the beginning of the third decade of the twenty-first century, the scale of the problems in the world of Barricades is overwhelming. As neglected problem-areas deteriorate rapidly and tensions escalate, there is serious doubt as to whether the barricades can hold.

22. NEW FRONTIERS

We have it in our power to begin the world all over again.
A situation similar to the present hath not appeared since the days
of Noah until now. The birthday of a new world is at hand.

—Tom Paine, 1775

Writing "Barricades" was a sobering experience for the entire team. We had been as realistic and conservative as we could in the development of this scenario, yet we had drawn a chilling picture of an increasingly divided world with anarchy enveloping society within our children's lifetime.

We then turned to the task of fully developing the alternative picture of the future, at that stage simply called "Scenario A." We had reached agreement about the general dynamics of this scenario, with dramatic economic growth taking place in the poor countries and new markets developing worldwide. The team had written significant parts of the story, and we had tested our conclusions against the best econometric and energy models available. But as we began to develop the heart of the story itself, it became increasingly clear that deep divisions were developing among the members of the team in relation to this scenario.

The gap was caused by the difference in our mental models—the deeply held internal images that we had about the way the universe is constructed and operates. Some of us saw the world through the eyes of modern physics: an interconnected web of relationships, with all matter constantly in motion and fundamentally open. Therefore, the future was not fixed. The world to us was full of possibilities for change and creativity. For the others, the Newtonian model seemed to prevail. This was a highly educated group of immense breadth. Most of them acknowledged modern physics, but only at an intellectual level. When it came down to doing the day-to-day work, it was apparent that their deeply held internal images of the way the world works were based on cause and effect, determinism, and incremental change. This deterministic view translated at times into a kind of cynicism—a skepticism and disbelief in the sincerity or goodness of human motives.

For example, early in our deliberations about Scenario A, in a plenary session with the whole team present, I proposed constructing a scenario that would project a vision of the kind of world that we would want our children to live in, a world order that was entirely plausible based on the driving forces that we discerned were at play in the world today. Why not develop this scenario, grounded in all of the knowledge and wisdom we had gained over the past two years, and then use the scenarios to help *create* the future instead of reacting to it? In other words, the actions of those who internalized the stories would, in fact, create the environment instead of merely responding to it.

This posed two significant problems for the team. In the first place, the Shell Group had always used scenarios to help their managers *respond* quickly to the changing business environment. This had served the Shell Group well, and had been a distinct source of competitive advantage since the early 1970s. But the concept of using scenarios to help *shape* the business environment was foreign to the mental models of many members of the team. Furthermore, the whole proposal seemed to them to lack business credibility. It was a naive approach and smacked of "do-goodism" and, even worse, of the theological.

As our work continued, the discussions about these issues dealt not only with the overarching theory of the scenarios, but with the substance of the stories and the practical aspects of gaining acceptance of the scenarios within the ranks of the senior management of the Shell Group. All of this was highly constructive and useful to our deliberations. But at points the conversations turned into debating sessions—sometimes quite vicious. As someone commented after one session, "A lot of blood was left all over the floor."

Those leading the opposition felt a sense of certainty backed up by their experiences in high positions both inside and outside the Shell Group. Their arguments were highly rational and supported by facts and figures. To them, this quantification was real. My arguments centered on "soft stuff": that we live in a relational, participative universe, that what is unfolding in the world is unique, and that this is an "open" moment in history. Under these circumstances, small discontinuities can suddenly and significantly transform the whole system. We have enormous opportunities to create something new. By building shared mental models, we can contribute to the environment we want to see unfolding.

At the time, I was doing a poor job of articulating these views. Ultimately, however, aligning the team around these issues became our greatest achievement. To develop real consensus, I felt we needed to share our mental models of how Scenario A might unfold—not only for the Group's use but also to help create a positive future for the world.

Two sets of events provided the nudge we needed.

The first grew out of our earlier decision in late 1991 to allow one of the key members of our team, Adam Kahane, to help South Africa make its transition from an apartheid society to a representative democracy. While we were in the early stages of developing our scenarios, a group of South African political leaders was struggling to find a common language to help them talk about the future. In part because of the work of Pierre Wack ten years earlier, they invited Adam to lead a scenario project to develop common mental models about the future of that country. When this invitation was received in our unit at Shell Centre in London, I talked it over at length with the key managers in Group Planning and in Public Affairs as well as with the Chief Executive of Shell South Africa. I felt this was an extraordinary opportunity for the Shell Group to provide crucial help in the delicate political process that was unfolding in South Africa, and strongly recommended Adam's participation. Adam was made available, and over the following eight months led that project, all the while maintaining his responsibilities as head of our sociopolitical economic unit.

The South African scenario team included twenty-two members from across the spectrum of South Africa's diverse constituencies. This multiracial group included left-wing political activists, right-wing separatists, officials of the African National Congress, trade unionists, mainstream economists, and senior corporate executives.

In a series of meetings in Mont Fleur, a conference venue near Cape Town, the team developed four scenarios, all focused on the nature of the political transition, the most important single uncertainty in the country. Whimsically, the scenarios were all named after birds.

In "Ostrich," the de Klerk government "sticks its head in the sand." Some path other than a free election is followed. White segregationist and black extremist groups gain in influence, stop communicating, and then polarize the country, leading to the "Lebanonization" of South Africa.

"Lame Duck" suggests what might happen in a prolonged transition with a constitutionally weakened transitional government. The government purports to respond to all, but satisfies none. Investors hold back, and growth and development languish amid uncertainty.

The third scenario, "Icarus," turned out to be the most important and influential. Proposed by some of the black members of the team, it suggests that a black government would come to power on a wave of public support and try to satisfy all the promises made during the campaign. It would embark on a huge, unsustainable spending program and consequently crash the economy.

"Flamingos" is the most positive of the four. Like "Lame Duck," it concerns a coalition government, but, as a pair, the two scenarios raise the question of what constitutes a "good" coalition. The name was chosen because when flamingos fly, they *rise slowly*, but they *fly together*. In this scenario, improvement is gradual and—most important—participatory. This is a plausible and consistent story of economic growth and political equality reinforcing one another.

At about the same time that we in London were locked in debate over how we were finally to tell the story of Scenario A, the Mont Fleur Scenarios were published and were being presented to the public and to the political, business, financial, and professional leadership in South Africa. They pointed to a vision for South Africa that began to influence the policy dialogue across the spectrum. For government and business observers, the existence of "Icarus" was reassuring because there was great fear in these circles about the possibility of the economy crashing in the wake of an unsustainable public spending program by a black government. For the left-wing black political parties, it was the first time that a team which included prominent members of the ANC and PAC seriously looked at the possibility of trying too much. It provided a nonthreatening way to bring the unpalatable message of "Icarus"—that a government policy of radically redistributing economic resources might not work.

Reports of the developments growing out of the Mont Fleur Scenarios had a significant effect on many members of our team. The events that were beginning to unfold in South Africa gave direct tangible evidence that scenarios could be used to positively shape the environment instead of merely helping people to respond more quickly to change.

The second set of events that heavily influenced the direction of Scenario A was our meeting with four highly respected and most remarkable men, all of whom spoke powerfully of their vision of a world consonant with the one we were describing in the scenario.

The first was R. Kaku, the Chairman of Canon, Inc. I had met with Kaku on a number of occasions and had been impressed with his breadth of vision. He was a true statesman in every sense of the word—a citizen of the world. Three influential members of our team and I went to Japan to discuss our emerging scenarios with the senior managers of our Japanese operating companies, and while there, I introduced our team members to Kaku and two of his senior managers.

We had a wide-ranging conversation with Kaku, which kept coming around to two principal themes. One was the need for radical reformation in Japan and the world. He mentioned a number of steps needed to achieve a kind of reform and began by saying:

> For the past fifteen years I have been calling for the establishment of an ethical state with a concrete plan for change. The first step is to give [Japan] a new purpose. Since our earlier objective of national prosperity has been achieved, we must now adopt a principle of "kyosei"—of living together in harmony and interdependence with the other peoples of the world—and commit ourselves wholeheartedly to this purpose.

Later the conversation shifted to his second theme—the role that corporations should play in an interdependent world. "Today," he said, "there is only one entity whose effort to create stability in the world matches its self-interest. That entity is a corporation acting globally." The essence of a successful company, Kaku asserted, is to strive to contribute on three dimensions: to its customers, to its employees, and to society. This is the essential element of the "spirit of Canon" and has been since its founding in 1933. This is the company's purpose, and it "forms the very backbone of our entire corporate complex."

Kaku said it had been his belief for many years that companies evolve through four stages. The first stage is purely capitalistic, which leads to labor-management conflicts. Overcoming these problems, the company reaches the stage where labor-management relations are based on shared destiny. All people in the company are treated as equals, thus narrowing the gap in income between executives and other workers. "Management with a common destiny invites all the parties to share their joys and sorrows as well as their prosperity." Few companies ever evolve to this stage. But, he said, overemphasis on this type of solidarity can create a gap between the corporation and society. So in the next stage, the company is considerate of its local community and makes contributions to it. He felt that several companies in Japan and elsewhere had evolved to this stage. But the company may eliminate the barrier between itself and the local community only to provoke friction at the international level. This eventually leads to the fourth stage where a company is committed to serving humankind as a whole through its philosophy and activities.

At its fiftieth anniversary, Canon made the decision to become the fourth kind of company. "Its responsibility is to address the larger conflicts in the world . . . the growing imbalance between the rich and the poor . . . to set up manufacturing operations in developing countries, to transfer technology, and to help them to become self-sufficient." The other global imbalance, which Kaku said was just as critical, is the depletion of the world's natural resources and the destruction of the environment. "Linked with this is the fateful question as to whether the deteriorating world will be able to feed its growing population and even be able to sustain life on earth. This is the vital imbalance between mankind existing today and what will exist in the future." The fourth type of company must be positively committed to the challenge of this overriding issue.

"I am convinced," he said, "that if the companies all over the world would join us in this quest, the world would be a vastly better place." By these measures, the role of business is becoming increasingly important. In the past, government provided the leadership. But, Kaku said, it was becoming clearer that in the increasingly borderless world created by a global economy, politicians and bureaucrats would not be the ones to turn to for guidance. It is the nature of politicians and government bureaucrats to serve one country. But global corporations can only do business in a peaceful and stable world. "It is vital for business to sustain peace on earth. If they do not assume a leadership role, who will save the world?"

The second critical conversation occurred in Argentina with Roberto T. Alemann, former Chairman and CEO of Ciba Geigy, Argentina; a former Economic Minister for Argentina under three presidents; and one of the most respected statesmen of that country. He spoke so eloquently and persuasively of the kind of world that could be created in Scenario A that I invited him to come to London to meet with Shell's Committee of Managing Directors and a few other very senior managers. A number of the members of our scenario team were also present on that occasion. That morning in Shell Centre he said of the Scenario A we were developing: "The lure of freedom and democracy cannot be extinguished—it is part of an irreversible parade of history. The people in the poor countries are leading the way in this revolution toward political and economic freedom. This push, this revolution, will fundamentally change the world."

The third was Harlan Cleveland, a former trustee of the American Leadership Forum and the former U.S. Ambassador to NATO who, drawing on a lifetime of distinguished service in the international arena, spoke to us about this "open moment" of world history and outlined a detailed strategy of what might be done to "make the world safe for diversity," where no nation or alliance will ever again be "in charge."

Finally, we had a long visit at Shell Centre with Kenichi Ohmae, the Managing Director of McKinzie & Company in Japan, and a highly respected, leading thinker on business issues. Ohmae spoke of the coming "borderless world," where economic interdependence could provide future global prosperity and peace.

⊷•◦•⊶

The reports back to us about the Mont Fleur Scenarios and the exposure to global statesmen caused the team's collective mental models to gradually shift. For almost a month we discussed, wrote, and rewrote the story of Scenario A. It was a tedious and exhausting process, but as we continued to talk together and consider all of the possibilities, we eventually came to a shared understanding of how the story should be told.

By June 1992 we were in the process of writing the final version of Scenario A, which we decided to call "New Frontiers." This title seemed fitting for a scenario of what can occur if the world embraces the unprecedented challenge of securing political and economic freedom for all people in the world.

THE NEW FRONTIERS STORY

In New Frontiers, the liberalization revolution continues and spreads on a very large scale. New Frontiers is a world where the center of gravity of the world economy shifts from the rich to the poor; and new priorities arise in the rich countries, reducing their consumption, which helps balance the extremely high demand and supply for almost everything throughout the developing nations. It's a story of new demands, new opportunity, turbulence, and vast change, resulting in governments and businesses being challenged beyond what they thought possible.

The most striking feature of the New Frontiers world is the dramatic economic growth in poor countries. From 1992 to 2020, the center of gravity of the world economy and of global business activity shifts from the rich world to the poor. At the outset of the scenario period, less than half the world's economy, in purchasing power terms, is in the poor world, while by 2020, it accounts for 70 percent. The incorporation of the big-populace poor countries—notably China and India—into the world economy is the most far-reaching change. Latin American reform continues to produce results; the decisive breakthrough comes when Brazil brings monetary and fiscal imbalances under control. The late 1990s are a period of very rapid growth in Latin America. Virtuous circles of development take place.

The successful economic reform contains the seeds of its own political stability. Reformists are reelected as their reforms bear fruit. In many cases it is the very poor, marginalized by previous policies, who are the strongest supporters of reform. The relationship between economic and political liberalization is different in different countries, but no matter what the model, individual freedom increases with successful free-market reform. Governments over time have learned to pay attention to the very poor. To avoid social explosions, they learn to spread the benefits of growth more equitably and to provide the necessary safety nets.

Progress in key countries such as Poland, Mexico, and South Africa inspires others through the "demonstration effect." Even in Africa, the hard grind of adjustment begins to pay off in the early twenty-first century, helped by a major breakthrough in hybridization introduced in the early 1990s, which multiplies the yield of cassava and sorghum, and makes them resistant to drought.

The former Soviet Union proves difficult to transform, but by the mid-1990s thousands of new enterprises have begun to sprout everywhere, and pockets of Russia are booming economic centers, their growth fed by foreign investment. By the turn of the century, the former USSR has passed the point of maximum crisis and can look forward to steady expansion.

In the rich countries, rising prosperity coincides with deteriorating public services, congestion, dirtier cities, rising crime, and pollution. This "paradox of wealth" causes a basic rethinking of the growth paradigm. Quality of life becomes a primary issue. Growth for its own sake is no longer sufficient. A public willing to spend money on the environment, infrastructure, and social goods such as education, health, and crime control, results in increased taxes, direct social spending by companies, and slowing growth and consumption.

The economic shift from the rich to the poor is accompanied by a power shift as it becomes clear that the poor countries can no longer be excluded from decision making. The diffusion of ideas, information, and capital crosses borders and cannot be stopped. The diffusion of technology, economic progress, and perceived mutuality of interests keeps poor countries from being marginalized. Many command a larger place on the world stage.

Developing a new international order is slow and complex and absorbs more and more time and energy of business people and business as well as governments, but a new order eventually takes shape. By early in the twenty-first century, India and Brazil hold seats on the United Nations Security Council.

A big step forward is the belated agreement on the Uruguay round of the GATT, which opens up liberalization in agriculture and services, and banishes the threat of trade warfare. Poor countries press on to remove the remaining barriers to trade, while the rich seek to reconcile environmental policy with trade. The momentum leads to launching the Bombay round in the late 1990s and to future rounds.

The new international order emerges because governments and individuals can see beyond narrow short-term self-interests to broader long-term interests and, in some cases, display a real generosity of spirit, as in the aid and debt relief extended to Russia and Africa to give them time to adjust.

Regionalism—a first step toward globalism—begins to flourish in the early years of New Frontiers. In East and Southeast Asia, regional integration led by business takes hold. Industrial development zones straddle national borders, such as Hong Kong, China, Taiwan, and the triangle of Singapore, Bataan, and Johore. Asia experiences the kind of boost from integration that Europe enjoyed in the fifties and sixties.

In Europe a widening range of trade agreements and security arrangements binds Eastern Europe more closely to the West. By 2015, Gorbachev's notion of a "European home" from the Atlantic to the Urals seems to be reaching realization.

Turkey is part of that "European home," but is also part of the Middle East and part of the network of economic and political relationships building up in central

Asia and the Black Sea. North Africa is linked increasingly to Europe through trade and gas pipelines, but also to the rest of Africa. Mexico is firmly integrated into the North American economy, and both are part of a wider, more liberal, Western Hemisphere trading area.

By the end of the scenario period, 2020, the world is a very different place. In many developing countries, success continues to breed success—better education has resulted in lower birth rates, economic growth has led to environmental reform movements, and greater economic liberalization has supported a drive toward democracy. Increased communication makes it easier to discover and discuss areas of common interest. In New Frontiers, rich and poor alike recognize their economic, social, and environmental interdependence.

The scenarios were published internally by the Shell Group in September 1992, following approval by the Committee of Managing Directors. Volume One contained the two scenario stories and their implications for the international order, economics and politics, energy and the environment, and business and people. Volume Two showed how those global themes might develop in different geographic regions and business sectors. It also quantified the global economic and energy implications of the two scenarios.

For the following twelve months, the scenario team traveled to more than fifty of the operating companies, meeting with their management teams for two- and three-day workshops. In these workshops, these scenarios were presented in unique and interesting ways to enable the participants to "live" in the scenario stories. This was followed by a series of facilitated strategy sessions designed to enable the managers to gain greater insights into how these alternative futures might unfold in their particular operating environment.

Our team was also privileged to be invited to meet with key government and nongovernment bodies in countries where the Shell Group operates. In these sessions we presented the scenarios and then held wide-ranging conversations with those present. In many instances, we would commence early in the morning, and the conversations would conclude long after lunch. These decision makers had to pause and reflect about alternative pathways our world may take at this important point in history. We also met with leading policymakers in the World Bank, the

United Nations, the International Monetary Fund, the Organization for Economic Cooperation and Development (OECD), the European Community, and the United Kingdom Foreign Office. In the United States, the Atlantic Council acted as a convener for a five-hour session in Washington, D.C., with fifty prominent government and business leaders.

That session took place in late June 1993, and was the last Shell scenario presentation I participated in. It was a fitting conclusion to almost four years with the Shell Group. We had accomplished an important part of the team's vision: "To inform the public dialogue." Our purpose in making these outside presentations was to help paint a picture for the people in leadership roles of what might be possible for the world at the beginning of this new era. From what I had seen during my work on the global scenarios, there are people in important places in all parts of the world who have in their hearts the wish to make New Frontiers a reality—to end the fragmentation in the world, and to create a better, more peaceful, more sustainable world for all.

⤛•✦•O•✦•⤜

It's much too early to judge the long-term impact of these scenarios on the Shell Group. But it is unquestionable that they are helping the Shell managers to gain significant new strategic insights for themselves and for the company—the feedback that the team and the planning coordination at Shell has received over the past few years has told us so. We have also learned that the scenarios have, over time, had a deep personal impact on many people. Two members of the scenario team itself have altered their respective career paths specifically to undertake the work of helping to create a New Frontiers world.

For me, personally, I can only describe my service on the scenario team as a profound aesthetic experience that was deeply satisfying to me. The whole experience served to underscore all that I was learning about the domain of generative leadership—how we can operate day by day to participate in creating new circumstances, new realities. Particularly over the last two years of our work together, I became acutely aware of how often the coincidences were occurring. Wherever I seemed to turn, the answers would be provided—a door would open, a "coincidence" would occur; someone would introduce us to another who "just happened" to know a person who, as it turned out, would provide a key direction to us. Sometimes the coincidences were very subtle reminders, and at other times the learnings came to us in intense waves. At times it was, to me, simply stunning.

Take, for example, our visit to Canon to meet with Kaku. Kaku himself was extraordinary. We were all struck by him—just being in his presence and being in dialogue with him was a singular experience. Immediately after that session, two of the senior officers of the company who attended the meeting took us for a tour of the headquarters facility, and in the process we saw a film that told the Canon story. During the course of the twenty-minute film, suddenly there appeared on the screen a familiar face—Bernard Cahier—the man whom I had met by happenstance at the Grand Prix at Monza back in 1977. He had directed me to the particular spot at the Curva Parabolica where I watched most of the race. It was there I experienced an early insight into energy fields and the collective state of flow—the same sort of field I had experienced in our meeting with Kaku just a few minutes earlier. I marveled at the synchronicity of it all.

Later, at lunch, the conversation turned to the subject of leadership, and I mentioned specifically to one of our hosts, Mr. Tadenuma, how striking I found Kaku's presence and his orientation of character, and how fully human he seemed to be. He was, I said, one of those people to whom I was drawn like a magnet.

Tadenuma said he completely understood. Then he told us an amazing story. In 1945 Kaku was only eighteen years old and working on a large ship in a shipyard in Nagasaki when the atom bomb was dropped. When he experienced the heat and force of the explosion, Kaku instinctively knew what it was, having studied physics and having understood the principles of nuclear fission. Although he was the junior member of the crew, he immediately led his fellow crew members deep within the hold of the ship and warned them it was crucial that they stay there and not become exposed to the contamination outside. He convinced them to stay in the hold of the ship for three days before they came out. Tadenuma said he believed Kaku emerged from this ordeal no longer the same person.

Since then, I've thought often about my encounters with Kaku and what Tadenuma said. Nagasaki had been Kaku's supreme ordeal, and he had emerged with, in Buber's words, "something more in his being." He not only epitomizes the servant leader, but he consistently focuses on the greater question of what we can create—how we can collectively shape our destiny. This, I have concluded, is what leadership is ultimately about.

23. A WORLD OF POSSIBILITIES

The ability to perceive or think differently
is more important than the knowledge gained.
—David Bohm

In February 1993 I was in Houston to present the 1992 Global Scenarios to the management team of Shell Oil Company. I thought of the meeting in Houston, years before, where I had made the brief comments to Norman Duncan that eventually led to my becoming the leader of the scenario team. Now, having presented the scenarios, I walked over to the Hyatt Regency Hotel to hear an address John Gardner was giving to the Forum Club of Houston. I entered the hotel ballroom, which was completely full.

John's address was entitled "Rebirth of a Nation." He gave, not uncommonly for him, an absolutely stirring talk that met with a standing ovation at its end. In his talk, he raised what he called the question underlying all the other questions today: "Whether we have it in us to create a future worthy of our past."

It was an inspirational talk—you could feel the energy he generated in that room. I was particularly moved by one passage. Speaking of America's free society, Gardner said:

> The surprising phrase, "We the People of the United States," suggested a source of legitimacy and power that was larger than the sovereign states and inclusive of the states. The words struck an enormously responsive chord in the emotions of most Americans—and the phrase spread like wildfire across Europe. In the older countries, weary of autocrats, the words were incredible and spine-tingling. Europeans were stunned by the boldness, the audacity of the Americans in coolly basing the legitimacy of their founding document on that astonishing phrase.

On the way back home to London that evening, I kept thinking of Gardner's central theme—creating the future—and the awesome power of those words, "We the People." I kept thinking about how we the people in fact *do* create the future through our declarations, our actions, our way of being. I thought about scenarios—how we paint word pictures and enter into dialogue with management teams and how (when all works as we hope it will) the future of the operating company is altered by the teams' changed perceptions and resulting actions. I thought about the Leadership Forum, what a highly abstract notion it was in the beginning. But out of the stories we told, and out of the commitment and actions of a small group of people grew something very tangible that had altered the life of a number of communities across the country. I thought about the law firm, and how when we were just a handful of young lawyers, only two or three years out of law school, we used to go on recruiting trips to all the best law schools. We would stand up before a group of one hundred law students and talk about our dream of a two-hundred-lawyer firm that would be a major force in the nation's legal community. We had a dream and the obvious commitment. Year after year, the best young lawyers were attracted to our small group, until ultimately, our dream was realized. We created our future that way.

This issue of how we collectively can create our future was at the very heart of the work we did at the Leadership Forum and with the scenarios at Shell as well. But we were not always explicit about it. It was difficult even to find the vocabulary to address the issue. The kind of transformation we sought to achieve with the fellows required a basic shift in how we thought and interacted. The changes that were necessary penetrated to the very bedrock assumptions and habits of our culture as a whole. But back then, I simply didn't understand enough about this subject to write or speak to it coherently. While I was at Shell, I did a little reading on the subject and kept up with the work of Peter Senge and his colleagues at the MIT Center for Organizational Learning. They were hard at work on these same issues: how people hold untested beliefs as private certainties; how the analytic model doesn't accept its contingent status—as Fred Kofman and Senge put it, "it adopts the face of necessity and claims universal validity"; and how what we see as "reality" is inseparable from our language and actions.

Bohm had spoken with me in London about the relationship between "reality" and language:

> The implicate order is in the first instance a language. It's not a description of reality but a language, an inner language, where you cannot associate each word to a thing. It's more like music. You cannot say one note means anything. It's like a painting. There are various spots of paint in an impressionist painting, but when you step back to see the picture, there is no correspondence between the spots of paint and what you see in the picture. Similarly, the implicate order and its mathematics does not directly come to describe a sort of correspondence with reality. It is simply a language. This language is referring to something that cannot be stated. The reality which is most immediate to us cannot be stated.

⋗⋅⬦⋅○⋅⬦⋅⋖

About two months after presenting the global scenarios to Shell Oil Company in Houston, I was in Paris for a business meeting. It was April and the city was beautiful. Mavis and the children were to come meet me for the weekend, for perhaps our last visit there for some time, because my assignment at Royal Dutch Shell was drawing to a close. The night before the family arrived, I was at a dinner hosted by the Global Business Network. Arie de Geus was there along with his close friend, Francisco Varela. Arie and others had told me for years that I must meet Francisco, that he was truly a remarkable person, but in the press of daily business, I had never followed up.

At the dinner I sat across from Arie and Varela, but it was too noisy to do more than exchange pleasantries. Then midway through the dinner, we were asked to rotate to other tables in order to ensure we were able to be with a variety of people. As I sat down at a new table, an American woman I'll call Catherine sat down next to me. She exuded a lot of energy, and I liked talking with her. She asked about my work at Shell, and when I told her about it, she expressed great enthusiasm and asked, "How did that happen?" I told her the story of Norm Duncan at the Lyceum and of how Renata Karlin then appeared in my life, of Mavis and her premonition of my working in London, and of the work at the Leadership Forum. I found myself telling her about the synchronicity of those early years at the Forum. It seemed natural to do so, and she fully understood. As we talked, our conversation rose to another plane. I told her I was deeply interested in the dynamics of how humans create the future together and I wanted to know more about the dynamic that occurs when doors seem to open for you in ways you could hardly imagine.

She said she was a doctoral student at Berkeley in the midst of writing her dissertation, which centered on these issues. She was in town to interview Francisco Varela, a distinguished professor of cognitive science and epistemology at the Ecole Polytechnique and the Institute of Neuroscience in Paris. It was only when she mentioned his books that it dawned on me who he was—the coauthor of such pathbreaking books as *The Tree of Knowledge* and *The Embodied Mind*. I had read these books while at Shell as part of my responsibility to keep abreast of new developments that could signal important change in the world. As a result, I was generally aware of the new "biology of cognition," a field of study that had been developed only over the past ten or fifteen years, about "knowing how we know." The central insight of the work of Varela and his colleagues on thought and perception was exciting and startling. The basic point is this: cognition is not a representation of the world "out there" but rather a "bringing forth of the world through the process of living itself." In particular, as humans, the only world we can have is the one we also create together through our language and interactions. Even more important, as these scholars point out, this very knowledge compels us to see that our world, our communities, our organizations will change only if *we* change.

Catherine and I talked at length about these concepts. Just before we parted that evening, she said, "If anyone can help you understand the dynamics of the phenomena of the doors opening, Francisco Varela is the one to do it."

The next day, I contacted Varela, and we arranged a time when he could meet me in London at Shell Centre. Our meeting took place about three weeks later, and I count it as one of the more important learning experiences in my life.

I invited Alain Wouters, a new member of our scenario team from Belgium, to participate in the meeting. Alain was one of the bright young stars in the Shell Group. Not only did he have a razor-sharp intellect, but he was wise beyond his years. He was one of those people to whom I was instantly attracted.

I began by telling Varela of my interest in learning about the dynamics of the "doors opening" or the "predictable miracles," as I had begun to think of them. I told him the story of what had occurred in my life since Watergate: a little of my old life; the crisis the divorce created; the subsequent trip to Europe, including the events at Monza; leaving the law firm; meeting Bohm and what I learned from him; and the synchronicity that began occurring after that meeting. I told Varela that I knew what had happened after that was real, but I was searching for some guiding principles, some way I could put my arms around this experience. I wanted to understand how we create our future, our world around us.

What followed was an eight-hour dialogue that seemed timeless. Alain and I both commented later about the field that seemed to form among us as we talked together. It was palpable and unmistakable—something I had felt so many times before.

The beginning point, Varela said, is to realize that what we are talking about is brand new territory—like exploring a new continent. Cognitive scientists are like sixteenth-century explorers looking at the early maps of America. "The maps are probably wrong in many respects, but at least we know the continent exists.

"Let's start," he said, "with what you learned from David Bohm—the open quality of the universe. All matter is constantly in motion and is insubstantial. The picture of a rock or a board or a human being as solid matter does not comport with reality. The notion that the world and our universe are made up of separate 'things' is an illusion and leads to endless confusion."

He said that there is also an emergent quality to the universe. You can have a group of simple components that suddenly act together "like an orchestra without a conductor" to give rise to something new, with quite different qualities. The work of Ilya Prigogine, the Nobel laureate in chemistry, contributed a great deal to our understanding of the emergent nature of our universe. "His work demonstrated the capacity for certain chemical systems—he named them 'dissipative structures'—to regenerate to higher levels of self-organization in response to environmental demands. Such emergent properties have been found across a wide variety of domains. In addition to oscillating chemical reactions, they've been found in fluid vortices, lasers, genetic networks, immune networks, neural networks, and ecosystems, as well as in social systems. All of these diverse phenomena have one thing in common: in each case a network of interacting elements gives rise to the emergence of a new entity with completely new properties. If you try to pinpoint the 'conductor,' it is nowhere to be found. You cannot pinpoint it."

This is a paradox, he told us. "You cannot understand it if you try to use classical thinking as a standard. David's way of expressing it is through the implicate order." I thought back to what Bohm had said to me: "The idea of the implicate order is that everything is enfolded in everything. Matter basically has its existence in the whole and manifests in a localized way rather than that its fundamental existence is made up of separate parts."

Varela continued: "Once you appreciate that the nature of our world, our universe, is nonsubstantial, yet exists, then you immediately open up to the possibility of change. It's almost a truism. There is an enormous opening for possibilities—possibilities to create and to change."

I recall Alain commenting at this point: "This is profound. I can see it now." Alain's thought processes were leaping ahead, and he was putting it all together even before Francisco had finished.

Varela continued by telling us there is another side to all of this. Since the world is open—nonsubstantial—the question arises, How do human beings experience it? "Unless we understand this," he said, "we cannot begin to understand how we interact with the world and how these 'predictable miracles' occur." The fact is, he said, "our language and our nervous system combine to constantly construct our environment. We can only see what we talk about, because we are speaking 'blind,' beyond language. Language is like another set of eyes and hands for the nervous system, through which we coordinate actions with others. We exist in language. It is by languaging and recurrent actions or human practices that we create meaning together. This is what I call the enactive view of knowing the world; we lay it down as we walk on its path."

He explained that a spoon is not something that exists in itself. It becomes a spoon in the background of our species (hands, food requirements, and so forth) and our human history (etiquette, national style, for example), both of them recurrent. We put the spoon to our mouth to feed ourselves. But for this recurrent practice, it would not exist for its present purpose. "This is the power of body and language—it can create recurrence of interactions and practices and thus create the future. There is an interaction followed by a response. Or we make a declaration or a promise, followed by a conditional satisfaction. That is how it goes."

He paused for a moment and then continued quietly: "We lay the path down by an accumulation of recurrent human practices. This is literally what it means to be human—to exist in a world of distinctions such as community, families, our work, and objects like spoons—all of which exist nowhere except in this accumulation of bodily actions and human practices, in this network of actions and languaging.

"Yet it's important to recognize this phenomenon is collective in nature. When I promise or make a request, I do so while in the midst of the past and current network of human practices. Although it is I who makes the request or the promise or declaration, it is not individual, because it is coming from and inserted into the whole background and history of human practices."

I didn't fully comprehend everything Francisco was saying to me, but as he spoke, I could literally feel a new understanding beginning to take place within me. It was not so much an intellectual dawning, but a more general "knowing," a more general coming together. One thing, however, was crystal clear: that what was being said to me was of fundamental importance. So later I took time to study my notes and the transcripts of the conversation, alone and, subsequently, with Alain.

As I considered the importance of language and how human beings interact with the world, it struck me that in many ways the development of language was like the discovery of fire—it was such an incredible primordial force. I had always thought that we used language to *describe* the world—now I was seeing that this is not the case. To the contrary, it is through language that we *create* the world, because it's nothing until we describe it. And when we describe it, we create distinctions that govern our actions. To put it another way, we do not describe the world we see, but we see the world we describe.

When I was talking with Francisco, he told me about how difficult it is to communicate all of this. "Our problem is that we hardly have the vocabulary or language to describe all of this—to talk about what it means to be human in this world." He said he draws on the Buddhist tradition in trying to explain this territory, but it took the Buddhists seven centuries to refine their language sufficiently, so it should not be surprising that those of us in the Western, scientific tradition are having some difficulty at this stage. "We can barely go beyond the metaphors here," he said.

Later in the day, we talked specifically about the events in my life, and he gave me his view of what had happened. He said that the shift that had occurred in me was not unique to me—it happens in human beings precisely because we are, like the rest of the universe, "open and insubstantial." Despite our habit of seeing ourselves as separate, solid "things," our minds, our beings are not fixed. We exist in a web of relationships.

There was a moment, he said, when all the "givens" I took for granted were dissolving. It was at that point that I was confronted with a world of possibilities.

"If there is an open, insubstantial system, we can create—why not? It is a paradox: confronting the lack of substance in the universe and in our lives is the source of our creativity. At this point, we have the integrity to be in a state of 'surrender.' It is in this state of being that we alter our relationship to the future and become a part of the unfolding universe."

As Varela spoke, I thought about the way both Buber and Greenleaf described the moment of commitment. This is the ground of being that enables the free will that is not "controlled by things and instincts" to operate. Francisco continued, "We take a stand and make a declaration to create a new reality. This is not an arbitrary statement, for in our being we have this inner certainty we can reinvent the world to this extent. We sense the time is right; the reality is already in the system waiting to be brought forth."

Part of the transformation that occurs in this circumstance, Varela said, is a declaration and a commitment that can only come from someone who has changed his stance from *resignation* to *possibility*. We need to learn how to internalize that capacity. "It's fundamental," he said, "yet we are still in the Stone Age when it comes to knowing how to consistently reach this state of being."

"What I want to describe to you next," said Varela, "is in the spiritual realm— spiritual because it has to do with human hearts. When we are in touch with our 'open nature,' our emptiness, we exert an enormous attraction to other human beings. There is great magnetism in that state of being which has been called by Trungpa 'authentic presence.'" Varela leaned back and smiled. "Isn't that beautiful? And if others are in that same space or entering it, they resonate with us and immediately doors are open to us. It is not strange or mystical. It is part of the natural order.

"Those that are in touch with that capacity are seen as great warriors in the American Indian tradition, or as Samurai in the Eastern tradition. For me, the Samurai is one who holds that posture in the world—someone who is so open he is ready to die for the cause. That capacity gives us a fundamental key and is a state of being known in all great traditions of humanity."

Later in the conversation, Varela warned, "There is great danger if we consider these people to be exceptional. They are not. This capacity is a part of the natural order and is a manifestation of something we haven't seen previously, not something we do not have. This state is available to us all, and yet it is the greatest of all human treasures.

"This state—where we connect deeply with others and doors open—is there waiting for us. It is like an optical illusion. All we have to do is squint and see that it has been there all along, waiting for us. All we have to do is to see the oneness that we are."

>-+*>-0-<*+-<

Just about every morning on my way to work in the Centre, I would stop by the river Thames and sit on a particular bench on the Albert Embankment that was my designated place to contemplate and relax. I would stay there for half an hour or more, just thinking, "being," and writing in my journal. My bench was under two beautiful trees near a small green called Jubilee Garden. The view from this particular spot was spectacular. Directly in front of me was the river with its boats getting under way for the day. And just across the river was Victoria Embankment, the broad and beautiful boulevard running between Westminster Bridge to my left and Waterloo Bridge further to my right. Just beyond Victoria Embankment was Parliament Street, Whitehall, and Downing Street. Off to my left, just on the other side of Westminster Bridge, was Big Ben and the Houses of Parliament. It was a historic and inspirational scene, identical to the view from my offices in Shell Centre, and one I never grew tired of.

During those early mornings by the Thames that spring and summer of 1993, I thought often about the fact that my assignment with the Shell Group was drawing to a close. In the days immediately after our meeting with Varela, this was particularly on my mind, and, while there was a real sadness that this important episode in my life was concluding, I was excited at the prospect of a new journey beginning. It seemed fitting that at this particular stage I should meet a person who could provide guidance and direction for the next stage of my life. Many of the lessons I learned from Bohm did not become clear until years later, as I reflected on my conversation with him in light of new experiences. So it seemed fitting in a way that some of the parts of the conversation with Varela were clear and that other parts left me with more questions than before, because I knew that the parts of our conversation that were still confusing would only gradually become clear to me as the next stage of my life unfolded.

24. CREATING THE FUTURE

Freedom and destiny are solemnly promised to one another
and linked together in meaning.

—Martin Buber

The Shell system of scenario planning is acknowledged to be one of the best state-of-the-art strategic planning systems used today. It has served the Royal Dutch Shell Group of companies extremely well over the past twenty years. In 1970, *Forbes* had said that Shell was the weakest of the seven major oil companies, even calling Shell "the ugly sister" of the so-called "seven sisters." Three years later, Shell discovered the power of targeting the mental models of its decision makers through scenario planning. By 1979, Shell and Exxon were seen as operating in a class by themselves, and by 1994, *Forbes* listed the Royal Dutch Shell Group of companies at the very top of their foreign Super Fifty—the largest companies outside the United States ranked by revenues, net income, assets, and market value.

When I arrived in London in 1990 to begin my work with the Shell Group, I had read everything I could find about its process of scenario planning. I thought I saw how the Shell scenario process fit right into the center of the quantum view of the universe that Bohm had described to me over a decade earlier. At that time, I also thought the Shell scenario process helped people to somehow sense and actualize new realities *prior* to their emerging, but I was mistaken. In fact, the process pointed to realities that were just manifesting in the world. Scenarios were being used in Shell to help their managers react almost instantly to new realities as they were emerging. This approach to scenarios is grounded in the deepest assumption that we human beings hold—that we cannot change things, so we must live our lives reacting to forces outside our control.

A central purpose of writing this book is to propose an alternative: if individuals and organizations operate from the generative orientation, from possibility rather than resignation, we can *create* the future into which we are living, as opposed to merely reacting to it when we get there.

At a level we cannot see, there is unbroken wholeness—an implicate order out of which seemingly discrete events arise, like the ink droplet in the glycerin that gradually manifests from its implicate state. All human beings are a part of that unbroken whole which is continually unfolding from the implicate and making itself manifest in our explicate world. One of the most important roles we can play individually and collectively is to create an opening, or to "listen" to the implicate order unfolding, and then to create dreams, visions, and stories that we sense at our center want to happen—that, as Buber said, "want to be actualized . . . with human spirit and human deed." Using scenarios in this way can be an extraordinarily powerful process—helping people to sense and actualize emerging new realities by providing a story for our time that, as historian Thomas Berry says, "answers the questions of our children."

The conventional view of leadership emphasizes positional power and conspicuous accomplishment. But true leadership is about creating a domain in which we continually learn and become more capable of participating in our unfolding future. A true leader thus sets the stage on which predictable miracles, synchronistic in nature, can—and do—occur.

The capacity to discover and participate in our unfolding future has more to do with our being—our total orientation of character and consciousness—than with what we do. Leadership is about creating, day by day, a domain in which we and those around us continually deepen our understanding of reality and are able to participate in shaping the future. This, then, is the deeper territory of leadership—collectively "listening" to what is wanting to emerge in the world, and then having the courage to do what is required.

>─◆>─○─<◆─<

As a result of the experiences recounted in this book, I began seriously studying the dynamics of predictable miracles. How was it that so many doors opened after I crossed the threshold by leaving my law firm? How was it that I "lost" the capacity to create the future I envisioned, and how did I regain that capacity? What principles can be discerned from these experiences and from connecting them to the profound new ideas that David Bohm, Francisco Varela, and others along the way shared with me? If this dynamic occurs in individuals, why can't it occur collectively in organizations and even societies as well? And, if so, what qualities of leadership will inspire this dynamic to occur?

I am the first to acknowledge that in trying to address these questions, we are exploring the frontiers of human knowledge and that whatever is said here is just a beginning. It is in this spirit I have set forward three fundamental shifts of mind necessary to the creative leadership I believe is so crucial for our future.

A FUNDAMENTAL SHIFT IN THE WAY WE THINK ABOUT THE WORLD

First, our mental model of the way the world works must shift from images of a clockwork, machinelike universe that is fixed and determined, to the model of a universe that is open, dynamic, interconnected, and full of living qualities. When Bohm talked to me about life in the bubble chamber, I had expected him to describe something similar to the schoolboy model of things, with particles, like tiny billiard balls, careening off one another. Instead, he described matter as sometimes particles, sometimes waves, sometimes mass, sometimes energy, all interconnected and constantly in motion. Once we see this fundamentally open quality of the universe, it immediately opens us up to the potential for change; we see that the future is not fixed, and we shift from resignation to a sense of possibility. We are creating the future every moment.

A FUNDAMENTAL SHIFT IN OUR UNDERSTANDING OF RELATIONSHIP

When Bohm explained the discovery of Bell's theorem and how it was confirmed experimentally eight years later, it simply affirmed for me all that I had been experiencing during my trip to Europe, in my encounter with the ermine, and later in Cairo. I saw the world as fundamentally connected. Everything that I have studied since that time has confirmed to me that *relationship* is the organizing principle of the universe. The physicist Henry Stapp describes elementary particles as "in essence, a set of relationships that reach outward to other things." The management theorist Margaret Wheatley writes that particles come into being ephemerally, through interaction with other energy sources. We give names to each of these sources—neutrons, electrons, and so on—but they are "intermediate states in a network of interactions." Once we see relationship as the organizing principle of the universe, we begin to accept one another as legitimate human beings. This is when, as Martin Buber said, we begin to see ourselves and others in an *I and Thou* relationship.

A SHIFT IN THE NATURE OF OUR COMMITMENT

In my old way of operating, I was very clear about my capacity to commit to something. Commitment meant being highly disciplined in sticking with something. I had been taught early on that "the way you win lawsuits is to make it happen—outwork the other person, stick with it, and stay deeply committed to what you are doing." This is the kind of commitment where you seize fate by the throat and do whatever it takes to succeed.

It was only later that I began to understand another, deeper aspect of commitment. This kind of commitment begins not with will, but with willingness. We begin to listen to the inner voice that helps guide us as our journey unfolds. The underlying component of this kind of commitment is our trust in the playing out of our destiny. We have the integrity to stand in a "state of surrender," as Varela put it, knowing that whatever we need at the moment to meet our destiny will be available to us. It is at this point that we alter our relationship with the future.

When we operate in this state of commitment, we see ourselves as an essential part of the unfolding of the universe. In this state of being, our life is naturally infused with meaning, and as Buber says, we sacrifice our "puny, unfree will" to our "grand will, which quits defined for destined being."

At the moment of my greatest challenge during the building of the American Leadership Forum, I completely lost sight of this principle. Once I saw what it meant to *surrender* in Buber's sense, I gave up my effort and striving, and gradually regained my balance. During this time, I began to understand, for the first time, the power of commitment.

PEOPLE GATHER

Out of this commitment, a certain flow of meaning begins. People gather around you, and a larger conversation begins to form. When you are in this state of surrender, this state of wonder, you exert an enormous attractiveness—not because you are special, but because people are attracted to authentic presence and to the unfolding of a future that is full of possibilities. This is what occurred when I gathered the trustees, founders, and others who were so important to the success of the Forum.

SYNCHRONICITY

Arthur Koestler, paraphrasing Jung, defines "synchronicity" as "the seemingly accidental meeting of two unrelated causal chains in a coincidental event which appears both highly improbable and highly significant." The people who come to you are the very people you need in relation to your commitment. Doors open, a sense of flow develops, and you find you are acting in a coherent field of people who may not even be aware of one another. You are not acting individually any longer, but out of the unfolding generative order. This is the unbroken wholeness of the implicate order out of which seemingly discrete events take place. At this point, your life becomes a series of predictable miracles.

>─◆─○─◆─<

Out of all of these experiences and my meetings with the remarkable people mentioned throughout this book, I have concluded that the leadership that can bring forth such predictable miracles is more about *being* than *doing*. It is about our orientation of character, our state of inner activity.

When we stand in this fundamentally open and interconnected state of being, we are like the Samurai warrior Varela mentioned, waiting expectantly with acute awareness for that cubic centimeter of chance to present itself. When it does, we must act with lightning speed and almost without conscious reasoning. It at this point that our freedom and destiny emerge, and we create the future into which we are living.

BRETTON WOODS
AND HADAMAR

We shall not cease from exploration
And the end of all our exploring
Will be to arrive where we started
And know the place for the first time.

—T. S. Eliot, *Four Quartets*

The final predictable miracle I will mention in this book was in many ways the most astounding of all. It seemed to bring me back to the very beginning of the circle, to my father and Watergate, and, at the same time, to confirm the nature of my work for the next phase of my life.

>―•―◦―◦―•―◦

I was working on the last two chapters of this book when I received a telephone call from Peter Senge's secretary at MIT. She was setting up a conference call among Peter, myself, and Betty Sue Flowers, the editor who had helped me with this book from its beginning as a series of reminiscences dictated into a tape recorder in the mornings after running, and who had later joined the team at Shell as editor of the scenarios and executive producer of the video based on the scenarios. Betty Sue and I had been meeting with Peter on a regular basis over the previous months to talk about the book and about what principles might be drawn from all that I had experienced. When Peter had us both on the line, he told us about a meeting that would take place in Bretton Woods, New Hampshire, a few weeks hence. It was to be a three-day gathering of about 350 people who had been actively engaged in creating learning organizations and communities. The intent of the gathering, he said, was to engage in deep conversation about what had been learned so far and what was now needed. Peter said he felt the conversations that the three of us had been having were "extraordinary" and that there was a "very particular energy" he felt as we talked together. The more we talked, the more we saw. He knew it was short notice, but he felt it was important that we both join him in a dialogue about the insights that were emerging from our work on the book.

We talked briefly about the format for the presentation. It would simply be an informal dialogue among the three of us late in the afternoon on the second day of the conference. We would not specifically plan what would be said—we would let it organically unfold. After we had talked about the guiding principles and had told some stories illustrating them, we would open up the conversation to include the audience. He felt it would all take about two hours.

We also talked about the significance of the conference taking place at the Mount Washington Hotel, the site of the 1944 Bretton Woods International Monetary Conference. The work of the delegates from the forty-four nations that gathered there had given the postwar world the currency stability that was badly needed for reconstruction. Peter said that whenever he went to the hotel, he felt the historical significance of what had happened in those rooms.

When I arrived at the Mount Washington Hotel, I looked at the plaques named after the world leaders who had worked there back in 1944. I stood in the Gold Room, where the accords that organized the World Bank, set the gold standard at thirty-five dollars an ounce, and selected the American dollar as the backbone of international exchange were signed. World War II had laid to waste every major industrial region of the globe except North America. President Roosevelt and his planners envisioned a postwar reconstruction—a new economic order—that would avoid the mistakes of Versailles, where the reparations and other conditions imposed on Germany caused such economic hardship that it created the political climate for Nazism. And Bretton Woods did create a completely different postwar world from the one created by Versailles.

On the afternoon of the dialogue, Peter, Betty Sue, and I met briefly to coordinate. Peter reiterated his feelings of expectancy about the moment, and his excitement about our being there together to engage in dialogue with this group. We sat silently for a moment, and then Betty Sue commented on the historic setting and the interesting timing of the whole affair: the following day marked the fiftieth anniversary of the convening of the original Bretton Woods Conference. What was so moving about Bretton Woods, she said, was how it had created a world in which the victors did not insist on revenge but treated their enemies as future partners.

An hour later, Peter opened the presentation by mentioning the fact that fifty years ago to the day, the delegates were gathering together in this very spot in preparation for the historic undertaking that unfolded. He commented that he didn't quite understand the full significance, but he felt that historic moment was somehow linked in meaning to what was to unfold at this gathering.

Peter then introduced me, telling of my background and the fact that I was now working with him and his colleagues at MIT's Center for Organizational Learning. He then introduced Betty Sue by saying that she had been an English professor at the University of Texas at Austin for many years and head of its Honors Program, the author and editor of many books, but that he had principally known her as one of the architects of the book and television series for Bill Moyers' *The Power of Myth* with Joseph Campbell.

At this point, rather than begin telling about the book itself, it seemed right to tell about how I met Betty Sue, because it illustrated beautifully one of the principles at the heart of the book. Back in 1989, when I had accepted my position with Royal Dutch Shell and decided to write this book, I knew that I needed some help. I would be too busy wrapping up at ALF and preparing to move to London to do all the editing work, and besides, I had no experience at all in writing a book. So I went on a search for an editor. I came up with a short list that included Betty Sue's name. One day I went to the library and pulled out the books these people had edited. I began to read through them to get a sense of the editors, but in the midst of trying to get through all of them, the name of Betty Sue Flowers kept coming to my mind. I couldn't get through all the other books because of this, so I got up from the table, went to the pay phone, got her number, and called her. I reached her at her office at the University of Texas and began telling her what I was up to. I gave her a two-minute summary of my story just to open the door. Then I was going to give her enough of the details so she would see the importance of the undertaking. I knew how well regarded she was because of the success of the Moyers/Campbell television series, and I felt in my heart it was going to be tough just to get my foot in the door. When I finished the introductory piece and before I could launch into the main explanation, she simply said "Yes, I'll do it. Let's talk about the next steps." I was dumbfounded, for once just speechless. But I recovered quickly, and we talked briefly about how I should proceed. She outlined all the steps I needed to take and told me the best process to follow in getting started. After I hung up, I went over to the library table and sat quietly trying to comprehend the whole thing. It was, in my mind, another of the predictable miracles. But it wasn't until much later, when I first met her, that I understood just how extraordinary this exchange was.

Then I turned to Betty Sue and asked her to tell the audience what had occurred from her perspective. At the time I called, she was in her office and very busy, with five people waiting to see her. Because of the success of *The Power of Myth*, she had gotten many, many calls from people who wanted help with their books. Because she couldn't possibly respond to all the letters and calls, she had made up a form letter to send out and a little paragraph for her secretary to read over the phone to people who wanted help on a book, saying that she simply didn't have time to work with anyone. "So why," she asked the audience rhetorically, "when a complete stranger calls out of the blue and wants you to do a book with him about something you don't fully understand, would you say 'Yes'? You say 'Yes' because something calls you to say 'Yes.' You cannot figure it out rationally, because if you try to figure it out that way, you would say 'No.'"

Betty Sue turned to Peter and asked if he had had many experiences like this. He replied that he had on a number of occasions. "It's like a magnet—you know that you were meant to do something together. This is for you, and you have to do it."

With that, I began to tell the story of my journey, beginning with the commitment to start ALF, crossing the threshold as I left my law firm in London, and meeting with David Bohm. I told the story of the doors opening one after another, culminating with the formation of the ALF board, and how this continued for more than eighteen months—until I lost that capacity. I asked what was it that allowed these helping hands to show up in my life, and then what caused them to disappear just as quickly. The three of us all pitched in, and the flow of the conversation led us to a discussion about destiny. Peter quoted Martin Buber's wonderful line "He must sacrifice his puny, unfree will, that is controlled by things and instincts, to his grand will, which quits defined for destined being."

It was at that point that a man in the audience joined the dialogue and asked about the role of the Supreme Being in all of this. He said he was a senior officer in a large corporation, and it was an "undiscussable" to mention matters of the Spirit or the Supreme Being in business. Yet it seemed to him that a conversation about such predictable miracles necessarily raised the question. Should we speak of God in the corporation, he asked? I thought for a moment and then told the story of my first presentation in Hartford to a group of potential founders of the ALF chapter there. After I concluded my remarks that day in Hartford, a member of the group stood up and asked me what the role of God was in all of this. He said I had spoken of servant leadership, alluding to service to mankind and service to something higher. "Where do you stand on this question?" he'd asked.

I gave a weak reply, not really knowing how to handle the delicate subject of God in a secular setting, particularly where I was dealing with senior people in the business world. The day after that encounter, I telephoned John Gardner and told him of my uncertainty about how to respond in this sort of circumstance. John simply said, "Over the entrance to Carl Jung's home in Switzerland is a Latin inscription: *Vocatus atque non vocatus, Deus aderit*—'Invoked or not invoked, God is present.'"

It's difficult, Betty Sue said, to find the language to talk about the life of the spirit in this secular world of ours. We need a language that brings us together about the deepest things we care about rather than pushing us apart. Peter said that a word he finds useful in talking about matters with the radiance of the Divine, beyond understanding or description, is "numinous." It's an acknowledgment that words and concepts no longer suffice, and that any attempt to articulate in any intentional way no longer suffices. "I've seen many times in dialogue sessions," Peter said, "when we literally could not find words to speak. In fact, the incredible imprecision and inaccuracy of words was full in the room—and we just sat there looking in silence at one another."

He went on. "It's funny, we sometimes think words are the measure, and somehow think that our ability to articulate is a measurable business. But it's precisely the immeasurable that we most deeply care about—the undefinable, the intangible, the inexpressible—the real. There's a wonderful section in Bohm's book, *Wholeness and the Implicate Order*, where he talks about the root of the word 'measure.' The western word 'measure' and the Sanskrit word *maya* have the same root. The word *maya* in Sanskrit is the most ancient word for 'illusion.' The prevailing philosophy of the East is that the immeasurable is the primary reality. In this view, the entire structure and order of forms that present themselves to us in ordinary perception and reason are regarded as a sort of veil—a veil that covers up the true reality which cannot be perceived by the senses and of which nothing can be said or thought."

Peter then turned to me and suggested that it might be useful to review for those present the lessons that I had learned from my experiences over the past twenty years or so that were the subject of the book. He said he felt it would be a good way to begin to consider the central question that was emerging in this conversation: How can we operate more consistently with the awareness that we aren't alone in this world?

I described the three fundamental shifts of mind that had emerged from my journey of predictable miracles—the shifts in how we see the world, how we understand relationship, and how we make commitments. I also talked about the results that grow from these shifts—the gathering of people and synchronicity.

When I had finished, and before Peter and Betty Sue could comment, a woman from the audience spoke up. A microphone was taken to her so she could be heard in the large room. Her name was Claire Nuer. She was from Paris and spoke in French, with her daughter Lara interpreting for us. Claire referred to the first and second fundamental shifts of mind I had described—that when our way of *being* shifts, our sense of identity shifts, and we see ourselves as connected to one another and to the whole universe. In this state, we accept others as legitimate beings, no matter what their race, gender, or national origin may be. Claire stood up and said very deliberately and forcefully, "This is a decision we can all take. We can put our minds to that service." When I heard this, I remained silent for a moment and then turned to Peter and Betty Sue and said, "What Claire has said brings up one of the core issues of the book, a theme we've only discovered in the last few weeks."

Peter explained, "The process we've gone through in working on the book has been quite extraordinary. Just when we think we understand the larger meaning of the book—just when we think we have seen it—then we continue talking, and all of a sudden a whole new level will start to appear. We thought the book started with Watergate and a deep inquiry about how we got to a point where a sacred trust which we all hold deeply precious could be so violated. It's not about criticizing an individual. The question is about the whole system. How did *we* get to this point? We thought Watergate was the starting place—but then we began to see a whole new level to this, and that's what Joe will describe to you now."

I began. "When my Dad was about thirty-five, he volunteered for the army and was in Europe just before the war ended. He was assigned to try the first war crimes trials, which set the precedent for the later Nuremberg trials. He supervised, planned, and was the chief prosecutor in two precedent-making cases, the Hadamar Trial and the case known as the Russelsheim Death March. He also supervised and prepared for trial the Dachau Concentration Camp case. In this capacity, he went into these camps or other facilities just as they were being liberated in order to gather and preserve the necessary evidence. And in this process, he saw the horror of it all."

When I got to this point in the story, I couldn't speak any further. I was suddenly and unexpectedly overcome by emotion. I sat there in front of those 350 people with tears streaming down my face. I was looking into everyone's eyes, wanting to continue—but I couldn't. The words wouldn't come. So I sat there just sobbing. It seemed like an eternity. The room was filled with silence. And finally, I began again, saying: "I was only eleven when I saw all that—" But I couldn't continue any further. Again the silence. Finally, a man I had met the previous day, Dinesh Chandra, came up on the platform. I stood up and he put his arms around me and held me. Dinesh is from India and heads his own company in this country. The moment I had met him, I had felt deeply connected to him, as if we were part of the same family. Dinesh continued to comfort and hold me until I was able to continue.

Finally, I went on. "In 1945, after the war was over and my Dad was trying these cases, my mother, my two sisters, and I would sit by the radio in the living room of our home in Houston and listen to the Sunday broadcasts where my Dad was describing what was occurring in these trials. Later he came home and told me he had put some files in his study and that I was never to go in there and look at any of that. He wanted that to be clearly understood. So the next day I promptly went to his study and looked at those pictures—the horror of what he had seen and what he had dealt with in those trials. So that's what I'm crying about," I told the audience. "Because it was so horrible and because he had to carry it with him all those years."

At that moment, at a deep level, I realized I was also crying my father's tears for all the victims and the horror. It was similar to the collapse of boundaries I had experienced in Cairo when I had spoken with my sister Claire over the telephone just after learning of the death of her son. Only this time, it was not terrifying at all. I very much felt my father's presence with me. And I felt the pain of the overriding question in his life: How could good people do such evil things? And how could we ensure it would never happen again? I began sobbing again, and it was the longest time before I could continue: "It was so horrible for him that he didn't want to think about it and couldn't deal with it for fifteen years. He then wrote a small book entitled *After Fifteen Years*. In the introduction, he said he was inspired to write the book in part because he hoped the questions that were asked in this book would have a lasting effect on the world and particularly on his son, who was just entering his second year of the practice of law. At Hadamar, for example, how could civilian doctors and nurses at a hospital murder hundreds and hundreds of innocent people—men and women and their children—who were brought into the hospital thinking the parents would be treated for some illness? How could doctors and nurses murder these people methodically just because they were Jews or Poles or otherwise different from themselves? How could it come to this? He wanted to know the answer. Here were people who went to church on Sunday, who were ordinary, law-abiding citizens, people sworn to serve and heal others. How could it be that they murdered, day after day after day, fellow human beings? What allowed people to do this? What were the dynamics that occurred in Germany to allow this to take place? And he said in his book: 'Watch out! It can happen here in America if we're not careful.'

"So my father dedicated his book to me, and in the process of my work with Peter and Betty Sue, I discovered that this is the work I intend to do. It is also the work Peter is doing: to discover how to transform institutions as well as the individual human heart to ensure that this kind of pain doesn't continue to occur in the world again and again. It's happening in countries across the globe and it's happening in its own form in companies and other organizations as well." I then began to tell the audience the story within a story that Peter had alluded to, the story of our discovering what the book was at its core.

"I discovered another level of what this book was all about a couple of weeks ago when Betty Sue faxed a letter to me from Germany. When I got the fax, I saw it was from Hadamar, Germany. A week later, when she arrived in Boston from Germany, I said, 'Betty Sue, I didn't want to say anything while you were in Germany because you were over there writing a book about love, but now that you're here, I have to tell you what Hadamar means to me.' Then I told her the story I just told all of you and showed her my Dad's book. Later Peter, Betty Sue, and I recognized that really my book starts much earlier than Watergate—it starts back at the end of World War II, when my Dad undertook his quest to understand how a whole system could create such evil."

When I finished speaking, Peter stood up and said, "Just to say the obvious, that's why we're here. Something special is happening here, and it's happening at many places all over the world. When the world leaders came here in 1944, they came with a sense of purpose and did extremely important work. And important work is taking place in this room at this very moment.

"If you think about what happened at the end of World War I, when people came to Versailles, and you think about what happened here at Bretton Woods in 1944, there was a profound shift. Claire said something this morning that still is ringing in my ears—she said, 'If we think fifty years into the future and imagine what choices we must have made today to enable that future, then this is the place we must come to make those choices and to do whatever we're called on to do in terms of the larger work. Now, Betty Sue keeps asking, 'So what's the next step? What's the next step?' That is the question for us all today."

The room fell silent again. After a few moments, I saw that Claire Nuer and her daughter Lara were making their way up to the front of the room to the speakers' platform. They were very close to me as they sat down. Lara held her face very close to Claire's, and her arm was holding Claire. In the other hand, she held the small lapel mike, in order to interpret for the others to hear. Claire's head was bowed as she began to speak directly to me, very softly, almost in a whisper. I could tell she was in great pain and overcome by grief. This was not surprising to me. As the story I had just told unfolded, I saw on the faces of those present a reflection of my deep pain. This had allowed me to go on. But the first words Claire whispered to me simply took my breath away. "My father died in Auschwitz." She paused for a long moment and took a deep breath. "It's incredible to me, that fifty years later I am sitting beside you at this moment. I have come to say to you thank you for making the decision to write this book and for sharing with us what you have said today." Again a long silence. Then she continued, "My father was born just a few miles from Auschwitz. His ten brothers and sisters lived near there as well. Now they are gone. Everything is erased, as if they all had never existed. Before today I thought the way to go on was just to surrender to it. But with what occurred today, things are better. The path we must go is now clear. My father had no degrees—he was a simple working man. Your father had many degrees and was a great lawyer. I feel their presence here with us today. Together, I feel they created the world. That's what I see as I sit next to you now."

She was quiet for a long few moments, then continued. "I did not have the time to come here this week from Paris. I had many, many conflicts presented to me from my business, but something was calling me to come." Then she looked up at me and said, "I now know why I was meant to be here today."

With that, Claire fell silent. We all sat there in that large room, all 350 of us. Not a sound was to be heard. Not a movement in the entire room. But the power of what was happening filled the space. It was one of the most compelling moments of my life. I felt the spirit of my father there very much with us all. I felt in that room with all those many people an intimacy, a closeness, a connectedness among us all.

Momentarily, Claire spoke again to Peter. She said that she had a videotape of something that she felt was important for those assembled to see. Would it be possible to have it played on the big screen on the stage so everyone could see it? The moderators met with the technical crew, and it was determined that it could be done. Within a short while the lights were lowered and the video was played. It was a tape Claire had shot of Auschwitz just a year ago. She had summoned the courage to go there after all this time in order to record the horror of that infamous death camp. The footage was beautifully shot. In surreal images, we saw the barbed wire enclosures, the guard towers, the gas chambers, the huge gas ovens. I sat there silently, sobbing from my gut as I watched the scenes which were underscoring all the grief and pain I had been feeling as I told the story of my father during the war.

But then at the end of the tape there was beautiful, soft music and the most surprising image appeared on the screen. It was an image of two birds, sitting on a slender branch of a tree in winter. Here's what was written there:

"Tell me the weight of a snowflake," a coal-mouse asked a wild dove.

"Nothing more than nothing," was the answer.

"In that case, I must tell you a marvelous story," the coal-mouse said.

"I sat on the branch of a fir, close to its trunk, when it began to snow—not heavily, not in a raging blizzard—no, just like in a dream, without a wound and without any violence. Since I did not have anything better to do, I counted the snowflakes settling on the twigs and needles of my branch. Their number was exactly 3,741,952. When the 3,741,953rd dropped onto the branch, nothing more than nothing, as you say—the branch broke off."

Having said that, the coal-mouse flew away.

The dove, since Noah's time an authority on the matter, thought about the story for awhile, and finally said to herself, "Perhaps there is only one person's voice lacking for peace to come to the world."

For the longest time no one in the room moved or said anything. The final words kept ringing in my mind: "Perhaps there is only one person's voice lacking for peace to come to the world." That, I thought, captures completely what the book is all about, what our work must be all about.

Finally, after the long silence, the moderator came up on the platform and closed the session by simply saying: "Invoked or not invoked, God is present."

NOTES

PART I: PREPARING TO JOURNEY

PREFACE

page ix C. G. Jung, "Synchronicity: An Acausal Connecting Principle," in *The Structure and Dynamics of the Psyche*, Vol. 8 of *The Collected Works of C. G. Jung*, trans. R. F. C. Hull (Princeton: Princeton University Press, 1960), p. 520.

page xii John of the Ladder as quoted in Henri J. M. Nouwen, *Reaching Out: The Three Movements of the Spiritual Life* (Garden City, NY: Doubleday, 1975), p. 9.

INTRODUCTION

page 1 Robert Greenleaf, *Servant Leadership: A Journey into the Nature of Legitimate Power and Greatness* (New York: Paulist Press, 1977).

page 5 Peter Senge, *The Fifth Discipline* (New York: Doubleday, 1990).

page 7 David Bohm, *Wholeness and the Implicate Order* (London: Routledge & Kegan Paul, 1980).

1. WATERGATE

page 24 See Leon Jaworski, *The Right and the Power: The Prosecution of Watergate* (NY: Reader's Digest Press, 1976).

page 25 John W. Gardner talked about "the laziness and self-indulgence of citizens" and "unscrupulous leaders" who "abuse the power entrusted to them" in his speech "Rebirth of a Nation," delivered to the Forum Club, 17 February 1993, in Houston, Texas.

3. THE JOURNEY BEGINS

page 33 Hugh Prather, *Notes to Myself* (Moab, UT: Real People Press, 1970).

4. FREEDOM

page 38 Richard Bach, *Jonathan Livingston Seagull* (NY: Macmillan, 1970), p. 77.

5. GRAND PRIX TEST RUN

page 45 For readers interested in learning more about the flow state, I recommend Mihaly Csikszentmihalyi, *Flow: The Psychology of Optimal Experience* (NY: Harper & Row, 1990).

6. THE ART OF LOVING

A book of penetrating insight for anyone interested in developing the capacity to love is Eric Fromm, *The Art of Loving* (NY: Harper & Row, 1956). Fromm says that love is not primarily a relationship to a specific person, but an attitude, an orientation of character that determines the relatedness of a person to the world as a whole.

page 47 "Bernadette" is a pseudonym.

7. ONENESS

page 54 W. Russell and T. Branch, *Second Wind: Memoirs of an Opinionated Man* (NY: Random House, 1979).

page 55 Martin Buber, *I and Thou*, trans. Walter Kaufmann (NY: Charles Scribner's Sons, 1970). For some passages, I prefer the translation by Ronald Gregor Smith (NY: Charles Scribner's Sons, 1958 [1952]).

pages 55-56 For readers interested in learning more about this expanded awareness, sometimes referred to as "unity consciousness," I highly recommend Ken Wilber, *No Boundary: Eastern and Western Approaches to Personal Growth* (Boston & London: Shambhala, 1979).

8. THE DREAM

page 58 Eric Fromm, *To Have or To Be?* (NY: Harper & Row, 1976). See pp. 108-109 for Fromm's discussion of freedom and the mode of existence symbolically represented by the hero.

page 58 Robert Greenleaf, *The Servant as Leader* (Newton Center, MA: Robert K. Greenleaf Center, 1973 [1970]). The essay I received in the mail was later reprinted in a collection of Greenleaf's essays, *Servant Leadership: A Journey into the Nature of Legitimate Power and Greatness* (NY: Paulist Press, 1977). I particularly recommend Chapter 11, "An Inward Journey," Greenleaf's own account of the fear and loss that is part of the journey toward personal transformation and servant leadership. Another of Greenleaf's essays which has wonderful insights about the journey is "My Debt to E. B. White" (Newton Center, MA: Robert K. Greenleaf Center, 1987). Greenleaf traces White's influence over a period of fifty-five years, especially White's capacity to "see things whole," an essential quality of servant leadership. All of Greenleaf's essays and his book can be obtained through the Robert K. Greenleaf Center, 1100 W. 42nd St., Suite 321, Indianapolis, IN 46208; Telephone (317) 925-2677; Fax (317) 925-0466.

9. CAIRO

pages 63-64 John W. Gardner, *No Easy Victories* (NY: Harper Colophon Books, 1968). Chapter 12 of this book is the most lucid and inspiring message about the need for community leadership I have ever read. It's as true today as it was twenty-five years ago.

page 66 John W. Gardner, *On Leadership* (NY: The Free Press, 1990), p. 199.

PART II: CROSSING THE THRESHOLD

11. THE MYSTERY OF COMMITMENT

page 73 Herman Hesse, *Demian: The Story of Emil Sinclair's Youth,* trans. M. Roloff and M. Lebeck (NY: Bantam Books, 1965), p. 108.

page 74 ". . . the box labeled 'too hard.'" I first heard this expression spoken by Admiral James B. Stockdale.

page 75 Rollo May, *Freedom and Destiny* (NY: W. W. Norton & Company, 1981). I recommend this book to anyone taking the inner path to leadership. May suggests that freedom loses its solid foundation without its opposite, destiny, which sets up the necessary creative tension and gives freedom its viability (p. 16). He also says that after pursuing our destiny for many years, we may arrive at a point where our freedom and destiny seem united. This was true of Martin Luther, who, when he nailed his ninety-nine theses on the door of the cathedral at Wittenberg, said, "Here I stand, I can do no other." Such acts, May points out, are "the fruits of years of minor decisions culminating in this crucial decision in which one's freedom and destiny merge" (p. 99).

12. THE GUIDE

page 77 *Sunday Times*, 27 July 1980.

page 77 David Bohm, *Wholeness and the Implicate Order* (London: Routledge & Kegan Paul, 1980).

page 79 Henry Stapp, as quoted by Gary Zukov, *The Dancing Wu Li Masters: An Overview of the New Physics* (New York: Bantam, 1980), p. 299.

13. SYNCHRONICITY: THE CUBIC CENTIMETER OF CHANCE

page 87 M. Scott Peck, *The Road Less Traveled: A New Psychology of Love, Traditional Values and Spiritual Growth* (NY: Simon and Schuster, 1978).

page 88 In addition to Jung's classic essay on synchronicity, see also F. David Peat, *Synchronicity: The Bridge Between Matter and Mind* (NY: Bantam, 1987).

page 88 This chapter benefited greatly from my reading of Arthur Koestler, *Janus: A Summing Up* (NY: Random House, 1978), pp. 265, 270. Also see in particular Chapter 13, "Physics and Metaphysics."

page 88 "all manner . . ." See the opening page of Part Four (p. 137) for the larger quotation from which this came.

PART III: THE HERO'S JOURNEY

The illustration summarizing the Hero's Journey is adapted from Joseph Campbell, *The Hero with a Thousand Faces* (Princeton, NJ: Princeton University Press, 1968 [1949]), p. 245.

14. THE MOMENT OF SWING

page 95 Ahmed Mannai rose from being a pearl diver in Qatar to an internationally recognized businessman with interests in fourteen countries. I first met Ahmed in London, just after meeting Bohm. My encounter with Ahmed at this early stage in the development of the Leadership Forum was very significant to me, another reflection of the "hidden hands" at work. In addition to providing important seed money, Ahmed also shared my vision of developing better leadership in the United States.

page 97 David Halberstam, *The Amateurs* (NY: William Morrow and Company, Inc., 1985), p. 40.

15. THE WILDERNESS EXPERIENCE: A GATEWAY TO DIALOGUE

page 100 My understanding of the history of the Outward Bound movement was developed during conversations with David Chrislip, Reola Phelps, and Eric Malmborg, formerly of the Colorado Outward Bound School. Also see Mark Zelinski and Gary Shaeffer, *Outward Bound, the Inward Odyssey* (Hillsboro, OR: Beyond Words Publishing, 1991), and Thomas James, *Education at the Edge: The Colorado Outward Bound School* (Denver, CO: Colorado Outward Bound School, 1980).

page 103 The phrase "one has been the context for the other" was taken from Joan Halifax, *The Fruitful Darkness* (NY: Harper San Francisco, 1993), p. ix.

page 104 This description was taken from a letter written by Arthur Walmsley, an American Leadership Forum Fellow and Bishop of the Diocese of Connecticut, published in *Good News: The Newspaper of the Diocese of Connecticut*, September 1987.

page 106 René Daumal's words can be found in the fragments of "A Treatise on Analogical Mountain Climbing" (1939), in "Notes Found among the Author's Papers," printed as a postscript in *Mount Analogue*, trans. Roger Shattuck (Baltimore: Penguin, 1960 [1952]), p. 115.

16. DIALOGUE: THE POWER OF COLLECTIVE THINKING

This discussion of dialogue benefited greatly from many hours of conversation with William N. Isaacs, the leader of the Dialogue Project at the MIT Center for Organizational Learning. See in particular Isaacs' article, "Taking Flight: Dialogue, Collective Thinking, and Organizational Learning," *Organizational Dynamics*, Fall 1990: pp. 24-39. Isaacs and his colleagues are investigating how to extend the extraordinary insights of Bohm, Buber, and others, and turn them into actionable skills and competencies. Isaacs' book, *Dialogue: The Art of Thinking Together* (forthcoming from Doubleday) brings together a decade of thinking by many people on this subject and explores different kinds of dialogue practice and its application at the personal, group, and organizational levels. See also Isaacs' chapter, "Dialogue," in *The Fifth Discipline Fieldbook*, eds. P. Senge, C. Roberts, R. Ross, B. Smith, and A. Kleiner (NY: Doubleday, 1994), pp. 357-64. In addition Peter Senge has written about dialogue in *The Fifth Discipline*, pp. 238-249.

page 110 David Bohm, "Epilogue" in *Unfolding Meaning* (NY: Doubleday, 1985).

page 117 Martin Buber, *I and Thou*, trans. Smith, pp. 8-9.

17. LESSONS: ENCOUNTERING THE TRAPS

Key insights about the Hero's Journey were provided by Robert J. Holder and Richard N. McKinney, "Corporate Change and the Hero's Quest," *World Business Academy Perspectives*, Vol. 6, no. 4, 1992: pp. 39-48.

page 118 Joseph Campbell with Bill Moyers, *The Power of Myth*, ed. Betty S. Flowers (NY: Doubleday, 1988), p. 121 ff. See also Joseph Campbell, *The Hero with a Thousand Faces* (Princeton: Princeton University Press, 1968 [1949]), pp. 101, 216.

page 118 For Greenleaf references, see notes for Chapter 8, p. 54.

page 119 Martin Buber, *I and Thou*, trans. Kaufman, p. 160.

page 119 Joseph Campbell, *The Hero with a Thousand Faces*, p. 216.

page 120 Martin Buber, *I and Thou*, trans. Smith, p. 109.

page 120 Joseph Campbell, *The Hero with a Thousand Faces*, p. 101.

18. THE POWER OF COMMITMENT

page 133 Martin Buber, *I and Thou*, trans. Smith, p. 59.

page 134 The Machado quotation was given to me by Francisco Varela.

page 134 C. G. Jung, *Memories, Dreams, Reflections*, ed. Aniela Jaffe, trans. Richard and Clara Winston (NY: Pantheon, 1961), p. 48.

page 135 Joseph Campbell with Bill Moyers, *The Power of Myth*, p. 120.

PART IV: THE GIFT

20. SETTING THE FIELD

page 149 Much of what Sheldrake said to me appears in *The Presence of the Past: Morphic Resonance and the Habits of Nature* (London: Fontana/HarperCollins, 1989). Also of great benefit to me was Margaret J. Wheatley, *Leadership and the New Science: Learning about Organization from an Orderly Universe* (San Francisco: Berrett-Koehler, 1992), especially Chapter 2.

page 152 David Bohm, *Wholeness and the Implicate Order*, p. 23.

21. BARRICADES

page 156 I first heard the term "hinge of history" from Harlan Cleveland during our conversations in London while the scenarios were being developed. Harlan, who was quoting Barbara Ward, used the term as a chapter title in his book *Birth of a New World: An Open Moment for International Leadership* (San Francisco: Jossey-Bass Publishers, 1993).

22. NEW FRONTIERS

page 160 The idea for the epigraph came from a conversation with Harlan Cleveland, who used Paine's phrase, "the birthday of a new world" as the basis for the title of his book, *Birth of a New World*.

pages 162-63 The Mont Fleur Scenarios were published in South Africa as a supplement in *The Weekly Mail* and *The Guardian Weekly*. The scenarios were later produced as a video.

pages 164-65 What Kaku said to me in our conversation he also spoke about at the Caux Round Table in Switzerland in 1991.

23. A WORLD OF POSSIBILITIES

page 172 John W. Gardner, "Rebirth of a Nation."

page 174 Bohm's words were taken from my transcript of our conversation in London, 1980.

page 175 H. Maturana and F. Varela, *The Tree of Knowledge* (Boston: Shambhala, 1991 [1987]). And F. Varela, E. Thompson, and E. Rosch, *The Embodied Mind: Cognitive Science and Human Experience* (Cambridge: MIT Press, 1991). In this context another important influence is T. Winnograd and F. Flores, *Understanding Computers and Cognition: A New Vision for Design* (New Jersey: Addison Wesley, 1989).

page 175 For an excellent discussion of language as a generative practice, see Fred Kofman and Peter M. Senge, "Communities of Commitment: The Heart of Learning Organizations," *Organizational Dynamics*, Fall 1993: pp. 5-23.

page 179 "Trungpa" is Chögyam Trungpa, author of *Shambhala: The Sacred Path of the Warrior* (Boston & London: Shambhala, 1988 [1984]). See especially, pp. 159-60.

24. CREATING THE FUTURE

page 181 Martin Buber, *I and Thou*, trans. Kaufman, p. 109.

pages 182-85 The reference to Thomas Berry and the way of expressing these insights about leadership were suggested by Peter Senge in personal correspondence, September 1995. Senge also made the same references in a keynote speech for a conference sponsored by Pegasus Communications, which was audiotaped as "Organizational Learning Infrastructures" (The Systems Thinking in Action Series). Bill Moyers quotes a similar passage from Berry in *The Power of Myth*, p. 139.

page 182 As we enter the third millennium, we are faced with increasing diversity, discontinuous change, and accelerating complexity. The philosophy described in this book will, I believe, enable us to meet these challenges. At the same time, however, we must continue to develop the traditional capacities essential to effective leadership. There are a number of authors and coauthors, many of whom have been mentioned in this book, I highly recommend to anyone seeking enlightenment along the path to organizational or societal leadership. They include Warren Bennis; James MacGregor Burns; David D. Chrislip and Carl E. Larson; Harlan Cleveland; Stephen R. Covey; Max Du Pree; John W. Gardner; Howard Gardner; Robert K. Greenleaf; Ronald A. Heifetz; Rosabeth M. Kantor; Peter Koestenbaum; John P. Kotter; James M. Konzes and Barry Z. Posner; Peter M. Senge; and Margaret J. Wheatley.

page 182 For those readers interested in a deeper understanding of our universe as one that unfolds according to a hidden, dynamic order, see F. David Peat, *Synchronicity: The Bridge between Matter and Mind* (New York: Bantam Books, 1987). The late Jonas Salk, who brought polio under control with the vaccine he developed, also spoke of a universe that unfolds kaleidoscopically according to a deeply ingrained order. He believed that people could develop the capacity to tap into this continually unfolding "dynamism"—that people can sense the way the future wants to unfold and can "hurry it along." "I have come to recognize evolution," he said, "not only as an active process that I am experiencing all the time, but as something I can guide by the choices I make. . . ." He said it was this force that guided him in the early 1950s to reject the common wisdom and develop a polio vaccine using killed viruses instead of live ones (*New York Times*, 24 June 1993, pp. 1, 9).

page 184 Henry Stapp, as quoted by Fritjof Capra, *The Tao of Physics*, 2nd ed. (Boston: Shambhala Press, 1985), p. 139.

page 184 Martin Buber, *I and Thou*, trans. Smith, p. 59. Reading Joseph Campbell's comment about the word "thou" and the reverence for the other that it suggests sharpened my understanding about why that word is so powerful. He said, "You can address anything as a 'thou,' and if you do it, you can feel the change in your own psychology. The ego that sees a 'thou' is not the ego that sees an 'it.' And when you go to war with people, the problem of newspapers is to turn those people into 'its'" (*The Power of Myth*, pp. 78-79). For additional insight into the I-Thou relationship, see Danah Zohar, *The Quantum Self: Human Nature and Consciousness Defined by the New Physics* (NY: William Morrow, 1990), pp. 128-32. Upon meeting another as our "thou," each becomes a part of something new, which is larger than itself (p. 132). See also Kofman and Senge, "Communities of Commitment."

page 185 Arthur Koestler, *Janus*, p. 259.

EPILOGUE: BRETTON WOODS AND HADAMAR

page 191 Martin Buber, *I and Thou*, trans. Smith, p. 59.

page 194 Leon Jaworski, *After Fifteen Years* (Houston, TX: Gulf Publishing Company, 1961).

INDEX

ABOUT THE AUTHOR

Joseph Jaworski began his professional career as an attorney with the Houston-based firm of Bracewell & Patterson. In 1975, he was elected a fellow of the American College of Trial Lawyers (the top 1 percent of trial lawyers). During fifteen of his twenty years with the firm, Jaworski was a senior partner and a member of the operating committee. He also helped to found United Savings Life Insurance Company (which later became Transport Life Insurance Company) and the Alaskan Oil and Refining Corporation (now Tesoro-Alaskan Refining Corporation). In addition, Jaworski ran a successful horse-breeding operation, Circle J Enterprises, which produced an American Quarter Horse Association Supreme Champion in 1972.

In 1980, Jaworski resigned from the law firm to found the American Leadership Forum, a nongovernmental agency responsible for developing collaborative leadership to deal with urban and regional problems in the United States. Ten years later, he was invited to join the Royal Dutch Shell Group of companies in London to lead a multinational team of experts in creating global scenarios—stories about the future of the world over the next thirty years.

After his four-year assignment with the Royal Dutch Shell Group, Jaworski joined the MIT Center for Organizational Learning, where he works with leading corporations to build learning organizations. Most recently, he has helped to create the Centre for Generative Leadership, a professional consortium that works collaboratively with clients to develop the leadership required to shape the future.

Jaworski's older son, Joe, is a lawyer in Houston. His other children, Leon and Shannon, live with Jaworski and his wife, Mavis, a physician, in the North Shore of Boston.

THE CENTRE
FOR GENERATIVE LEADERSHIP

The Centre for Generative Leadership (CGL) is a professional consortium that works collaboratively with clients to develop the leadership required to shape the future in our current environment of fundamental change and spiraling complexity. CGL offers expertise in

Large-scale transformation

Strategic management

Leadership development

Scenario and systems thinking

Joseph Jaworski is a founder and chairman of CGL, whose partners have worked for Fortune 50 and Fortune 500 companies as well as for governments and nongovernmental groups in more than forty countries on every continent.

For more information, contact the Centre for Generative Leadership at (508) 468-7097.

BERRETT BK KOEHLER

I F YOU LIKE the ideas in *Synchronicity* and are interested in joining with others to explore them further, please fill out the form below and mail, fax, or email the information to:

Berrett-Koehler Publishers
450 Sansome Street, Suite 1200
San Francisco, CA 94111
Tel: (415) 288-0260
Fax: (415) 362-2512
Email: bkpub@bkpub.com

Name _____

Title _____

Company _____

Address _____

City/State/Zip _____

Tel _____

Fax _____

Email _____

Where did you buy this book? _____